AT HOME IN JAPAN

AT HOME IN JAPAN

A Foreign Woman's Journey of Discovery

Rebecca Otowa

TUTTLE PUBLISHING
Tokyo • Rutland, Vermont • Singapore

Published by Tuttle Publishing, an imprint of Periplus Editions (HK) Ltd.

www.tuttlepublishing.com

Library of Congress Cataloging-in-Publication Data
Otowa, Rebecca.
  At home in Japan : a foreign woman's journey of discovery / by Rebecca Otowa. -- 1st ed.
    p. cm.
  ISBN 978-4-8053-1078-6 (hardcover)
1. Otowa, Rebecca. 2. Americans--Japan--Biography. 3. Wives--Japan--Biography. 4. Country life--Japan. 5. Japan--Social life and customs. 6. Japan--Biography. I. Title.
  DS832.7.A6O86 2009
  305.813'052186092--dc22
  [B]
                              2009018554

ISBN 978-4-8053-1078-6

Distributed by

North America, Latin America & Europe
Tuttle Publishing
364 Innovation Drive
North Clarendon, VT 05759-9436 U.S.A.
Tel: 1 (802) 773-8930 Fax: 1 (802) 773-6993
info@tuttlepublishing.com
www.tuttlepublishing.com

Japan
Tuttle Publishing
Yaekari Building, 3rd Floor
5-4-12 Osaki, Shinagawa-ku
Tokyo 141 0032
Tel: (81) 3 5437-0171 Fax: (81) 3 5437-0755
tuttle-sales@gol.com

Asia Pacific
Berkeley Books Pte. Ltd.
61 Tai Seng Avenue #02-12
Singapore 534167
Tel: (65) 6280-1330 Fax: (65) 6280-6290
inquiries@periplus.com.sg
www.periplus.com

First Edition
14 13 12 11 10   10 9 8 7 6 5 4 3 2

Printed in Singapore

Front Cover © Datacraft/imagenavi/Getty Images
Cover Design by Daniel Urban
The endpaper design is taken from an old kimono originally owned by the author's mother-in-law.

TUTTLE PUBLISHING® is a registered trademark of Tuttle Publishing, a division of Periplus Editions (HK) Ltd.

Contents

This book is dedicated to my family.

Acknowledgments

This book grew and changed considerably in the six years since I began it. At times I doubted my ability to finish it, but there was always someone to put me back on track. I am indebted, in life as in writing, to the support of the Association of Foreign Wives of Japanese. Many past and present members actively helped me during the writing, particularly Kathy Ono (for proofreading, comments, and dauntless encouragement), Deirdre Merrell (for friendly suggestions and invaluable networking), Wanda Miyata (for being there), and also Winnie Inui, Pam Uchida, Jessica Goodfellow, and Daya Oka (for fellow-writer support) as well as many others. If I have left names out, it's my "miss", as we say in Japan. Heartfelt thanks also to Sandra Kimball, my mentor, who trusted me to trust myself during the difficult last phases. I'm grateful to Eric Oey, for believing in the project, and Bob Graham, Genna Manaog, and Levi Christin for tireless editing of the essays and sensitive treatment of the tricky illustrations. Finally, I'd like to thank my husband, who has been my one-man cheer squad, always applauding and encouraging every new thing I try.

*My home on an unseasonably cool
and cloudy summer day
Late July, 2003*

Introduction

For almost three decades I have been the housewife, custodian, and chat-elaine of a 350-year-old farmhouse in rural Japan. These two elements—the farmhouse, and Japan in general—have been inextricably bound with my life, and I owe my life, as it is now, to them.

I came to Japan in 1978 as a university student, self-centered as the young always are, with an exaggerated confidence in my paltry store of knowledge, undercut with a pervading suspicion that I didn't know as much as I thought I did. Indeed, the more I learned, the more my ignorance seemed to grow. In subsequent years, as wife of the heir of the house, daughter-in-law of his mother, mother of the next-generation heir, and responsible resident of the village, I got a concentrated dose of Japanese culture, society, and psychology. From all sides, Japan nudged me and pushed me and pummeled me to assimilate it. There were times of pain, the pain of being forced into a mold I felt I couldn't fit into, and the contrary pressure of knowing that I was essentially nothing more than a link in a centuries-old chain of this family. Every day, as I lived in Japanese rural society, thoughts and views I had held from childhood were challenged—notions of space and time, beauty and truth; meanings of words, gestures, and expressions; assumptions of my worth and my rock-bottom right to be whatever I was. Why did I, a product of a young and free society, put up with it? I've asked myself this many times. The only reason that made sense was that it was my promise and my destiny. And however painful it may have been, the act of taking up these challenges and facing them squarely gave me back the very truth, beauty, meaning, and worth I thought I had lost.

Perhaps the most important thing I learned was that growth always and only results from a willingness to change one's thinking and entertain a different point of view. Japan has helped me grow—it has been a crucible of maturation for me. In this book, as I have described the house, village, and lifestyle, I have also recounted my struggles, my misgivings, my compromises, and my mistakes. I want to express my gratitude for the rich, intense, and varied tapestry of experience I have been given in this tiny microcosm of Japan. I want to give myself a hearty pat on the back for the years of endurance that have led to this space of reflection and this time of rewards. Finally, I want to honor my house, the ancestors who kept it up and passed it on, floating it like an ark down the years, and all those who, in this modern age, find delight in the treasures and traditions of the past.

This book traces a circular path, from the basic physical details of life in the house and village, through relationships with family, neighbors, and the natural and supernatural entities with whom I share this space. Then it bends back toward my inner life, to touch on some of the pivotal memories of my life here, the lessons in perception that Japan has taught me, and finally, an examination of the ways I have been changed by living here—and the places in my heart where I find I have resisted change. Each subject has provided me with a chance to muse upon my Japanese coloration—how deeply dyed I have been, where and when the dyeing process stopped, or whether it in fact continues to this day.

My experiences are not unique—they may not even be very unusual. But I hope that among the readers of this book, those who know Japan may find something to love here, and those who dream of making their home in another land and culture may be able to see a rough map of the terrain that they may find in their souls, and gain some courage for their adventure.

Welcome to my world, my house, and my life.

The House

I first saw my home in an old black-and-white photograph, forming the background to a family group of stern father, preoccupied mother, and self-conscious kids. My boyfriend Toshiro was showing me the album of his childhood. The house was a member of the family. It spread its wings of benevolence and security over the heads of the people in the picture.

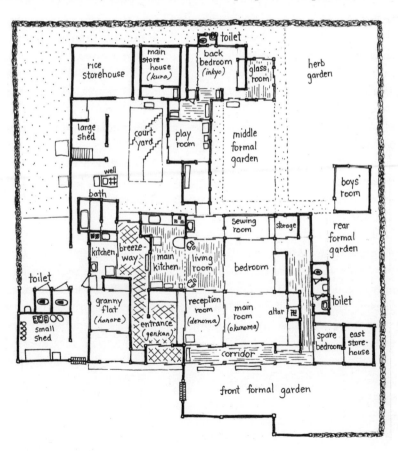

Soon afterward, I was invited to the house for the first time. I had known Toshiro only three months; we were students in Kyoto, an hour's drive away. We sat on *tatami* (thick woven straw mats) in cool, dim, spacious rooms where doors flung wide let in the piercing insect white noise and intense green of Asia. Toshiro's mother sat serenely in her own environment, her legs sprawled comfortably to one side, cheerfully chatting in the local dialect. We walked in the fields and his father picked a watermelon. We swam in the pond and wrote wishes on stones, tossing them into the water. My wish was to live in this house, married to this man.

The house is set on a big lot facing south, slightly raised above the road. A large vegetable patch in front, a small herb garden at the back, and three formal gardens surround the rambling collection of buildings. The oldest part of the house is a square of four rooms surrounded by wooden verandas, sliding glass doors, and deep eaves, with other rooms of varying age attached to this main core. All the buildings are raised on stumps above the ground with a crawlspace beneath for ventilation. Considering the size of the house, the "walls" are very few. Most room partitions are paper, wood or glass sliding doors that can be removed to create a larger space.

The property is surrounded on west, north, and east by high hedges, and open to the south, where the view from the front door is of the road crossing the river and curving upward through trees. Although we have neighbors on three sides, there is no window through which a neighbor's house can be directly seen. The sense of seclusion is strong, even though our house is one of about a hundred in the village.

My house is proud of its long life and its role of protecting the family through fifteen generations. My husband was born on its tatami, and he first saw his mother's face against the backdrop of its wooden doors. Yet it welcomed a stranger like me, and wrapped me round in its benevolence. From the beginning I never felt that it resented the know-nothing foreign wife. It knew my heart, and over the years I have come to know its heart. It's a friendly heart, and an accepting one.

Life at Home

Futons airing in our front yard

Shimenawa
decoration

Beginnings

I t's New Year's Eve. The house is as clean as we can make it. The *o-mochi*
(glutinous rice cakes) have been pounded, shaped, and placed in positions
of honor. The family altar and the shrines to the household gods have been
decorated with flowers, fresh leaves, candles, incense, and miniature bottles
of *sake,* according to the preferences of the various deities. The final bath
of the year, and the *toshi-koshi soba* ("year-crossing noodles"), have been
enjoyed. The air is filled with the spicy scent of the *sakaki* leaves used for
purification. The ceremonial envelopes of money sit ready for distribution to
neighborhood temples and as gifts for relatives' children.

As soon as the midnight countdown is complete, family members wish
each other Happy New Year in the traditional phrases, and make the round
of the household shrines, clapping and bowing and silently wishing all the
things everyone wishes every New Year. Some of us make the snowy trek up
to the local shrine and sip *sake* (rice wine) around a bonfire, smiling with
other well-wrapped-up villagers, cheeks red and eyes bright in the firelight,
watched by the ancient trees.

New Year's morning is leisurely, beginning with a ceremonial meal of *o-zoni* soup, *sashimi*, roasted dried plums, traditional delicacies, and more sake. Each food is a wish for long life, health, and happiness. Then we spend the day around the *kotatsu* table, reading New Year greeting cards, eating mandarin oranges, playing games, watching TV, and napping. The Beginning has been reached—we have breasted the tape of another year. The family is together, we are all fine, we can look ahead to the future. It is a moment for reflection and for gratitude.

The Japanese are people who like to mark the occasion. New Year is just the largest and most universal of all the ceremonies of Beginning variously enjoyed and endured, especially early in the year. The first snowfall of the year, the first dream, the first plum blossom, the first putting of calligraphy brush to paper—the list goes on and on. Endings, too, are clinched with ceremony. I learned quickly (though getting used to it took longer) that even the smallest neighborhood cleanup, even the most minor Women's Association meeting, even the most ordinary music rehearsal—even parties!—must begin and conclude with a few words and a bow of solemnity. The exact moments of beginning and ending are decided by an exquisite attention to timing that I have yet to master after a quarter century of living here.

These rituals are mind-numbingly boring in most cases, but I suspect that, for the Japanese, they are comforting as well. If we foreigners chafe at the excessive ceremony in this culture, Japanese people abroad must feel all at sea, paralyzed with indecision in social situations because they can't tell when the moment of beginning or ending has come. In our international marriage, these are gifts we can give each other—the security of time-honored ceremony from my husband and the welcome relief of casual relaxation from me.

Recently I have started to feel the attraction of rituals myself, as a way of giving meaning to the transitions of life. Now, in our house, I have devised my own little New Year's Eve ceremony. Sometime in the evening, amid the bath and the meal and the traditional observances, we all sit down and write letters to the selves we will be next New Year's Eve. We also open and read the letters we wrote the previous year. These letters are private and for our own eyes only. Each family member has now amassed quite a collection of them, allowing us to reconnect with our past selves and providing a pleasant feeling of continuity. This ritual has become important and worthwhile, and I am pleased to have made my original contribution to the torrent of ceremony.

And so begins another year in my corner of Japan.

Chopsticks and chopstick rest (hashioki)

Feasting

Food, glorious food! There is an ardent and ongoing love affair with food in this country. Everywhere you travel, there are regional delicacies to sample and also to bring home in attractive gift boxes. Neighborhoods are crammed with restaurants, bistros, and eating places of all kinds. Turn on the television and there will be the inevitable reporter, sitting down at some table somewhere, engulfing a mouthful of something or other, his reaction—"Mm!", a gulp, and a breathless "Delicious!"—instantly transmitted to eager viewers. Food is offered to the gods and ancestors, food is exchanged during gift-giving seasons, food is decorated and garnished and pampered like a celebrity. Most of all, food is enjoyed—by everyone.

When I think about the changes in Japanese food culture in the years since I first came here, it is hard to believe I'm still in the same country. These days, the old-style markets, with their strangely colored lighting and hand-lettered signs, air-conditioned to the point of refrigeration and smelling strongly of fish, are becoming quite rare. Instead, supermarkets are huge and the range of products is amazing. No longer do I have to make the semi-desperate journeys to small, cramped imported food shops in Kyoto to engage in shoving matches with other foreigners for the last package of walnuts or bottle of green Tabasco. I can get what I want most days, in most places.

The increasing sophistication of the supermarkets mirrors that of the general public. With increased travel to far-off destinations, more people can now demand Beaujolais Nouveau or debate the quality of tiramisu. Even average housewives are known to venture into such culinary exotica as cheese making or meat smoking. It's getting much harder to awe my neighbors with talk of unusual foods. When I mention linguine or tarragon or tequila, I now get nods of recognition instead of stares of incomprehension.

Surprisingly, what *does* awe my Japanese friends is to hear about my own forays into traditional culinary arts. Housewives who practice the ancient art of pickle making are definitely thinner on the ground these days—and as for pounding o-mochi in a wooden mortar at New Year, our house is one of only a dozen or so in our village where the rhythmic thumping can still be heard. I'm proud of my hard-won ability to serve as o-mochi turner, stooping next to the mortar and, with wet hands, quickly turning the hot mixture between blows of the huge mallet. Timing is crucial, in the alternation of pounding and turning, so that my hand doesn't end up as a colorful o-mochi ingredient.

I was also schooled by my various female in-laws in the art of setting up the formal dinners that accompany memorial services for deceased family members. On two square trays holding a total of ten to a dozen dishes for each person, the fare—fish, tofu, and vegetables—is arranged in time-honored configurations, and beautifully garnished with flowers and leaves reflecting the season. The cooking itself is a challenge of more complexity than I could possibly describe, and in any case my main job, as keeper of the house, is not so much cooking as the preparation of the vessels and utensils. Each place setting contains up to twenty separate ceramic or lacquer dishes, multiplied by perhaps a dozen guests; these must be brought out of their wooden boxes in the storehouse ahead of time and washed before being filled and arranged on the trays. And of course, the process is reversed after the meal. The kitchen becomes a hurricane of dirty dishes, food leftovers, splashed sake, hot soapy water, steam, and damp dishtowels as the cleanup is performed at breakneck

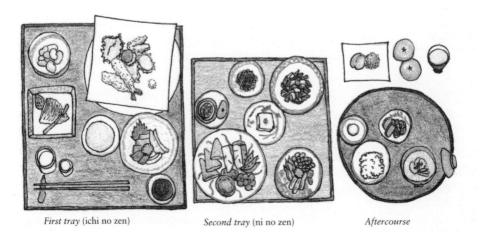

First tray (ichi no zen)   *Second tray* (ni no zen)   *Aftercourse*

Formal dinner, memorial service, January 2000

speed by a phalanx of female relatives. (Cooking and serving food at home, and all attendant chores, are exclusively feminine occupations; in our area at least, men never get involved unless there is an enormous potential for back-slapping and congratulation.) No wonder the Japanese word for feast *(go-chiso)* contains the character for "running around frantically".

It is exhausting—the scurrying, the scalded fingers, the backaches from stooping, the headaches from trying to think of fifteen things at once. In traditional Japanese hospitality, the hostess's strenuous exertion is as much a part of the feast as the raw fish and the sesame tofu. It is like an invisible sauce that flavors everything, and this is expected and applauded. I feel it as a kind of marathon-style meditation—a switched-on mode that I maintain all day until there is nothing left to be done. A more intense contrast with my usual switched-off, solitary, weekday lifestyle could not be imagined. Of course, variety is the spice of life as well as of food and, without the frenetic pace of hospitality, we couldn't fully appreciate the deep drenching peace that falls over us as we walk slowly back inside after seeing off the last guests. Whew! I can relax until next time, and each next time gives me a little more confidence. I can do this—and it earns me the respect of my in-laws and neighbors, which is not so easy to come by.

The aroma of miso soup, with the sound of chopping green onions, is a powerful evocation of Home and Mother to Japanese people.

The Kitchen

The kitchen is the most emotionally charged room in the house for a Japanese wife. It's her workplace, her arena, her sphere of creativity, her classroom. Here is where she stands at the sink, with a child leaning against her watching her chop vegetables. Here is where she washes dishes through a blur of tears after being scolded by her mother-in-law. Here is where she breathlessly arranges her *piece de resistance* on a beautiful serving dish before carrying it out for all to enjoy. And here is where she sits, a cup of tea before her, listening to the sound of guests in the front room who are due to leave soon, and will need to be bowed out.

Around the world Japanese cuisine is famed for its ingredients, its cooking methods, and its presentation. The ingredients are usually seasonal, very fresh, and cut into many different shapes. The cooking methods may be absurdly simple—two minutes in boiling water—or hugely complicated, involving intricate combinations of flavorings and finicky adjustments to pot coverings, water amounts, and temperature. The presentation, possibly the most important element of all, is a delicate symphony of color, spacing, and garnishes. One way or another, all these miracles are performed in a kitchen.

I worked in just such a kitchen for twenty years, of which five years were shared with my mother-in-law. Two women in the same kitchen is a difficult situation. Anything can become a battleground, from chopping and scrubbing techniques to utensil arrangement and food preservation. My mother-in-law's teaching task was formidable: I was not only from another family but from another country across the world, my ignorance seemingly bottomless. Furthermore, my otherwise adequate command of Japanese didn't extend to arcane culinary terms delivered in the local dialect. As the crowning obstacle, I am left-handed, so that everything I did looked "funny" to her and she despaired of ever teaching me proper kitchen ways. At the same time, I disliked her habit of leaving leftovers in pans all over the place, to be reheated time and again, becoming more salty and peculiar-smelling with each repetition. Both of us were hugely relieved when she had her own granny flat built and we could each have our own kitchen.

I also ran up against some age-old prejudices. The kitchen is not a place for outsiders, not even the men of the family. In one of our more memorable arguments, my mother-in-law said it made her sick to her stomach to see my husband, or my two sons, Goki and Yuki, working in the kitchen. Since I had no daughter, it was up to me to perform the kitchen tasks singlehanded. As I ploughed through the daily round, I often thought of my dad, who regularly washed the dishes and often cooked, and wondered how my sons would take care of themselves when they went out into the world.

What are the differences between a Japanese kitchen and a Western one? When I first came to live here, I had only two burners on the stove, with a built-in grill (for fish) but no oven. Since Japanese food is designed to wait for the guests, not to be waited for, a housewife can prepare many dishes beforehand; but when I cooked Western meals it was often a struggle to bring everything hot to the table. The sink and work spaces were much lower—barely up to my hips—because women here tend to be much shorter. And, depressingly, the kitchen in a traditional house is usually dark, cramped, and situated well away from the "best" rooms, which are reserved for guests. I tried to relieve the darkness by painting the walls (which were not old, just particle board), so that they were sometimes pink, sometimes green, sometimes cheery salmon and turquoise.

In recent years, some things have changed. The kitchen area of 1950's vintage was much newer than the rest of the house, the result of a modernization project undertaken by my father-in-law for the benefit of the firstborn son's wife (me). I'm glad he never found out that I hated it. A few years ago, I was finally able to remove the white-flocked ceiling and fake wood veneer walls of that earlier renovation, and to restore the original high ceiling with the smoky bamboo latticework and beautiful massive beams that had been hidden all along. I now have both dishwasher and oven, and my stove now sports three burners. The sink and countertops have been raised to a more comfortable height—my sisters-in-law are always cheerful in offering help when they visit, but now have a bit of a stretch to reach the taps. Glass tile skylights and big windows brighten the north-facing kitchen, which is now contiguous with the living room when we remove the dividing doors in summer. It's still a place of hard work and strong emotions—but now my three men work there cheerfully alongside me, helping me clean and trying out new dishes—and it's my own kitchen at last.

Stool and bucket used in a Japanese bath (o-furo)

In the Bath

One evening I spent a grueling couple of hours crawling between the young corn plants, muddy to the elbows, yanking out the huge soft summer weeds and packing earth around the corn stalks. As I trudged home on exhausted legs through the humid, mosquito-humming twilight, there was only one thought in my mind. Soon I was settled up to my neck in fragrant steaming water, with a sigh of gratitude for the healing power of *o-furo*—the Japanese bath.

It seems odd that even on numbingly hot, humid summer days, when sweat springs out on the body at the slightest movement, a deep hot bath can be just as welcome as in the dead of winter. This is a tribute to the centuries-old Japanese genius for hydrotherapy that has become famous around the world. To the Japanese, bathing isn't just a matter of washing the body. It's a process of renewal on many levels, from the physical through the mental to the spiritual.

The traditional o-furo takes place at night. The nighttime bath is a perfect transition between the day's activities, challenges and problems, and the soothing abandonment of sleep. As such it feels completely different from the modern morning shower, with its agenda of gearing up for whatever the coming day may bring. The bath may also have an element of recreation, and can even be a vacation destination, as witness the enormously popular hot spring resorts all over the country.

There is also the element of ritual purification, which is deeply embedded in the culture, having its origins in the native religion of Shinto, and manifesting itself in countless ways. The love of whiteness—of paper, rice, bread, young girls' skin; the elaborate roofed basin at the entrance to a shrine, surrounded by people waiting their turn to rinse their hands and mouths before praying; the *sumo* wrestler tossing handfuls of salt into the ring before a bout—all are symbols of the national quest for purification.

In the olden days, the Japanese bath was a social event. In villages such as ours, where heating a large quantity of water was expensive, several households would take turns providing the bath, with each person washing himself outside the bathtub (which was more like a huge iron pot over a fire pit). When he was clean, he would enter the tub for a refreshing, deep hot soak, in water which was used by everyone. Naturally there was a certain order to bath usage: older before younger, guests before householders, men before women. This order reflected both the Confucian ethic of respect for the elder and high-status person, and the Shinto idea of woman as less pure than man. "Unclean" women were relegated to a lower place in the bath line. The housewife herself took the *shimai-buro* (final bath).

When I stayed with a host family in Tokyo as a student, I, the Guest, was usually invited to be first in the bath. I realize now that the family was offering the highest degree of hospitality, but at the time I had no idea. Also, I couldn't understand why the wife of the house kept calling me to the bath and insisting I get in at a certain time. What was the rush? I didn't realize then that the bathing hierarchy was an integral part of family life. When I became a housewife myself, it was borne in upon me that the wife has to wait for everyone else to bathe before she can do so, thus it is in her interest to keep the procession moving as smoothly as possible. At holiday times in our house, when relatives came to stay and there were many people ahead of me in the bath line, I would often be so sleepy by the time my turn came that I gave up

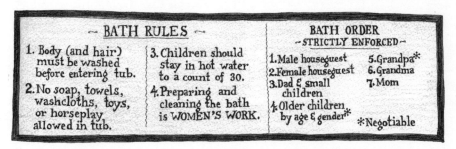

~ BATH RULES ~		BATH ORDER ~STRICTLY ENFORCED~	
1. Body (and hair) must be washed before entering tub.	3. Children should stay in hot water to a count of 30.	1. Male houseguest	5. Grandpa*
		2. Female houseguest	6. Grandma
2. No soap, towels, washcloths, toys, or horseplay allowed in tub.	4. Preparing and cleaning the bath is WOMEN'S WORK.	3. Dad & small children	7. Mom
		4. Older children, by age & gender*	*Negotiable

Bath rules as I understood them as a young wife.

on my bath entirely and went to bed instead. Jumping the queue was not tolerated, as my mother-in-law emphasized on the few occasions when I tried it. I suppose, having recently graduated from last place herself, she felt obligated to make sure I was aware of the rule. As the final bather, it was my duty to let out the water, open the windows, clean up the mess, rearrange the shampoo bottles, and so on, after everyone else was done. The *shimai-buro* position was not an enviable one. Besides all the work, soaking in water already used by the entire family was not exactly a purifying experience. As in many other aspects of life, the housewife got the leftovers.

The bath is a lot less stressful these days, with only my husband and me. He is quite easygoing about the order of our bathing, and doesn't mind my getting in first if he is going to be home late. Returning from a bout of heavy weekend gardening, we often get into the bath together. I guess it's no coincidence that my enjoyment of the bath has increased as the hierarchical power-play aspect has decreased (although we still revert to the traditional Bath Order when we have guests in the house). These days I sometimes wonder why this simple daily activity should have been the source of so much emotional turmoil in my early days in this house. In a way you could say my concept of the bath has itself been purified, and brought back to the basics of purification and renewal. I am grateful. It feels good.

Hooking Up

The village is fast approaching the end of an era—big changes are on the horizon. The first little signals are already appearing along the streets and lanes: the fat black snakes of pipe, the orange and white traffic cones emblazoned with names of construction companies, the white sandbags like pillows flumped down in the road. The village of Otowa is about to get a sewer system.

The construction, so far, is unobtrusive, carried out by diminutive purple steam shovels and polite, soft-spoken workmen who never whistle at girls or even take their shirts off. Posted signs apologize in advance for the inconvenience, which will be considerable for families whose driveways have only one exit onto a narrow lane. But in spite of mutterings about increased taxes, no one has protested the march of progress.

For centuries, village waste was handled by two methods—the wayside ditch and the earth toilet. Wash and bath water flowed down to a canal which ran largely underground and eventually joined the river. Human waste, as in China, was long regarded as a valuable source of garden fertilizer. When I first came to live here, it was still a common sight to see grannies on their way to the vegetable patch with "honey buckets" suspended on sticks from their bowed shoulders. I myself was no stranger to this homely substance, as it became my duty to monitor the big concrete tanks under our three toilets and call the night soil truck when they got full.

No longer. The sewer system, which has been slowly creeping eastward from the town over the past ten years or so, has finally reached our village. Soon some of the most ordinary sights, sounds and smells of daily life will become memories to be recounted to incredulous grandchildren. At this moment I can hardly imagine the ways my life will change. The noisy and aromatic night soil truck, with its huge cylindrical tank coiled with yards of mud-colored vacuum hose, will disappear. I will no longer need to worry, when I visit the toilet, that the car keys or loose change in my pocket will be dislodged and fall into the unspeakable murk. Summer worries about vermin, especially mosquitoes, will be a thing of the past.

Another thread connecting us to our animal roots will snap. Good-natured country-style jokes will cease to be heard, as this earthy and universal human function recedes beyond the pale of everyday conversation. What will the first-grade children do with their cast-off baby teeth, if they can no longer observe the picturesque custom of throwing lower teeth over the toilet roof (so they will grow upward) and upper teeth down into the tank (so they will grow downward)? Everything will be altogether cleaner, more sanitary, more colorless. Unwanted substances will be whisked into the void of "away", gone forever, unrelated to us as, free of responsibility, we step forward into our Brave New World lives.

Do I sound sarcastic? That's because I have mixed feelings about this giant step toward modernization. Universal sewerage is not necessarily the most efficient or environmentally friendly way to solve the problem of human waste in the countryside. As with universal electricity or universal Internet connections, or any other trends toward centralization, I worry a little about a possible breakdown of services. Right now, each household could handle its own waste if it was absolutely necessary—after all, there's a lot of land around us. With connection to the sewer system, this option will disappear.

Well, there's no halting progress. Good-bye to the familiar old toilet pit, filled in by the cute purple steam shovel (see right). Good-bye to an era.

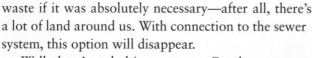

Comfort

In some ways we are a very modern family. We speak in English—and we speak our minds. We go online. We take advantage of technology—all of us have cell phones, though they sometimes don't work in the house. But in one important area, we are a real old-fashioned Japanese family. In winter, when we are all at home, we gather in the living room and spend our free time sitting around the *kotatsu*.

A kotatsu is a low table with a blanket or quilt spread over it and a heating device inside. In old houses like ours, the area under the table is often actually sunk into the floor, so the legs can stretch out and the feet can rest next to the little heater. It's not quite as universal as it used to be, what with the advent of heated floors and carpets, but it still occupies a prominent place in the Japanese heart.

Efforts have been made to modernize the kotatsu. Of course the heat source is now electric, replacing the traditional bed of coals which sometimes resulted in fire or asphyxiation. The patterns of the quilts have changed too. Several decades ago, designs were unapologetically loud and cheerful, with bright reds and yellows predominating, while modern quilts are more understated in brown and beige. Rectangular kotatsu, circular kotatsu, even kotatsu the height of a dining table with chairs—all have made their appearance. But the essence doesn't change: the casual, comfy, knee-rubbing, foot-bumping, snack-eating, cat-dozing, intimate coziness of it.

The kotatsu is for family, not for guests. It's hard not to feel like a member of the family if you are close enough to be invited into the kotatsu room, surrounded by drying laundry, the odd stack of newspapers or mail, mandarin oranges, teacups, and the whiff of kerosene stoves and whatever was for lunch.

So many memories of Japanese are grounded in this humble piece of furniture. As children, they hide in it with just their heads poking out to watch TV or play games. As students, they do their homework at it or snooze with the familiar quilt pulled up to their chin. As dads, they retreat behind the newspaper with a hand reaching out now and then for another mandarin. As moms, they file their nails or write a postcard, savoring the relaxation after the usual hectic evening of Doing for the Family. As old grannies, they knit. As grandpas, they just sit and warm their bones.

Winters are so cold, and the house is so old and drafty, that we naturally gravitate to the warmest room in the house, conveniently situated with phone,

TV and kitchen close at hand. Weekends in particular will find us all around the kotatsu, companionably engaged in our own projects, with regular meal-time hiatuses when everything is cleared off the table (yes, we even eat at the kotatsu). Photo albums, handwork, Scrabble, comic books, vegetable cuttings, mild disputes over TV programs or videos, phone conversations—this is a multi-purpose space indeed. When the snow is deep, except for bath and bed, what better place could there be?

It's not really possible to keep the original architecture of the house and to have an efficient heating system at the same time. I had to make the choice—and I chose to be true to the old style. So, even though our kitchen and living room were remodeled several years ago, winter is still a time of struggle with kerosene stoves and rooms that are just a couple of degrees above chilly. But one thing hasn't changed. We still have our snuggly, comfortable kotatsu to cheer us and keep our family together all winter long.

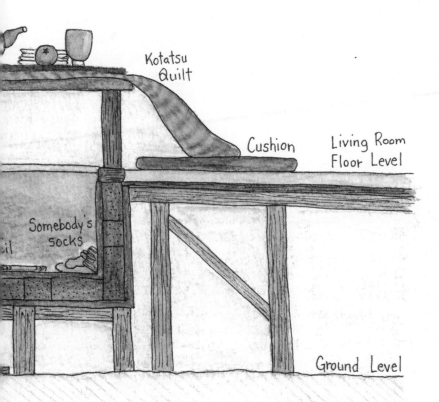

The universe of the kotatsu: *a cross-section*

Sleep

My husband doesn't enjoy sleep. He sees it as a waste of time that could be spent in more productive activity. I'm not sure if his attitude is shared by Japanese people in general, but in this as in other areas, stoicism prevails; there is little notion of optimum sleep hours, and lack of sleep is disregarded, especially in times of intensive group work.

I haven't yet despaired of converting him to my own view: that sleep is not only a luxurious self-renewing portal between one day and the next, but also a doorway into different realities, a precious opportunity for tapping into the direct, wordless wisdom of dreams. Because I think sleep is so important, I've poured a lot of energy into improving our sleep environment. We began, some twenty-five years ago, with a typically stoical Japanese sleeping arrangement—double-size futons stuffed with cotton batting, and pillows filled with buckwheat husks. We soon decided to make some changes, and the pillows went first. I got sick of laying my head down on what felt like a sack of pebbles every night, and replaced them with the kind of feather pillows I remembered from my childhood, imported from the US. We persevered with the futons for some years, but finally acquired inner spring mattresses, which changed our sleeping life forever—although when guests come, they sleep on futons, the most comfortable we can manage.

One of the more arcane lessons I received from my mother-in-law was the art of futon-making. The most difficult step was placing the cotton batting in layers on top of the inside-out futon cover, and then turning the whole thing right side out. This was a sweaty and irritating procedure, involving much huffing and puffing to manhandle the heavy batting inside the cover, and was usually done outside, because wisps of cotton filled the air and covered our garments. But the result was worth the trouble: a gorgeous, soft bed fit for a king. Alas, over several years, these lofty futons grew progressively harder and thinner and turned into *senbei-buton* ("rice-cracker futon") as they are jokingly known. Re-fluffing the inner cotton batting (*maru-arai*, "entire washing", which is done by professionals) does work for a while; but in the end, of course, the pressure of sleeping bodies flattens all the air out of them once more.

The Japanese climate is so humid that periodic airing of bedding is a necessity. My mother-in-law decreed that if the weather was fair and I would be home all day, the futons should be hung out at 10 a.m., turned at 1 p.m., and brought back inside at 3 p.m., after energetic whacking with a carpet beater or stick (I use a badminton racket) to get the dust out. This precise timing is an example of the finely calibrated nature of traditional Japanese housekeeping, which I suspect is now being eroded as wives get busier. On a fine, warm day, the southern faces of huge, multistory apartment blocks are festooned with a cheerful patchwork of futons and blankets hanging from the balconies, giving a new meaning to the phrase "bedroom community". In the countryside, the futons are spread on the roof or hung on special poles in the yard. Some people find these futon-draped neighborhoods vulgar or unsightly, but I like them. There is a homespun, comfortable, personal quality to it that is a bit like sleep itself. We are all vulnerable in sleep, and watching a loved one sleeping makes us feel affectionate and protective toward them. When we expose our futons to public view, we are unconsciously admitting our vulnerability, and our membership in the family of humankind.

In the multi-functional traditional house, any room can be made into a bedroom simply by laying futon on the floor. The paper sliding doors that make up the walls transmit every sound, and especially in smaller town houses, young couples must perfect the art of silent lovemaking. My mother-in-law bedded down with her small children, and her husband had his own room, to which she would repair after the kids were asleep. Our own family sleeping arrangement was the popular *kawa-no-ji*, in which mother, baby, and father are lined up like the three vertical strokes of the character for *kawa* (river). When my boys were babies, I was happy to have them right next to me, for easy care and feeding at night. Although modern trends of family life have given older children their own rooms, I don't think there is much likelihood of Japanese babies ever being consigned to lonely cribs in solitary rooms, as in the West. The "skinship" value of communal sleeping, for them, overrides any fear of children absorbing unhealthy influences from parental intimacy.

Since our house has no heating or air-conditioning at night year-round, we feel the changing seasons most intensely in bed. In winter, we curl under thick pre-warmed blankets and a huge down duvet, pulled right up over our heads. Crowded in with stereophonically purring cats, we snooze all night in our cocoon of bedding, to emerge, reluctant butterflies, into the predawn icebox of another work day. In this winter reality of carefully orchestrated comfort, it's impossible to recall how blissfully easy sleep was six months before. Summer nights, with windows thrown wide to let in the fragrant, frog-singing air, we lie stretched on our backs like royalty, relishing each faint breeze, often with no bedclothes at all. The cats have deserted us to seek night excitements; getting up at 5 a.m. on weekdays is no hardship, since daylight is already here. Even with the ever-present mosquitoes, I vastly prefer the summer environment. But winter or summer, we have heavenly, natural silence and glorious total darkness to lull us to sleep. In this, as in many other ways, we are blessed to live in the countryside.

Family and Neighbors

Village O-Jizo shrine next door to our house

Traditional charm (o-mamori) *for a safe journey*

A Sentimental Journey

How do we feel when we hear the word "family"? For most of us, the associations of this word begin in childhood with Mommy, Daddy, brothers and sisters, and sometimes grandparents. In adulthood, however, many of us experience a shift in consciousness, so that when we are asked "Do you have a family?" we realize that the people who make up our family are now completely different. We have a husband or wife, sons or daughters, and they have become our family. There is no particular moment when that shift occurs. We feel it gradually, as a background to our day-to-day thoughts. It is a mysterious process.

Even more mysterious is the event that could be called the beginning or kernel of this shift in consciousness—the meeting of a man and woman who will eventually get together and have a family of their own. Although the imperceptible motions, wobbles, and vacillations of our choices throughout life may seem random, at some point we can look back and see that there were subtle but inevitable steps leading to that momentous crossing of paths. The odds against meeting "The One" seem very slim, and utterly based on chance; how much slimmer, indeed, when The One is growing up in another country across the world, completely outside our awareness.

In 1955, in California, Disneyland and I were brought to birth only a few months apart. Surrounded by orange groves, suburban bungalows, palm trees, funky motels, and brightly colored cars with huge fins, I grew, moved and circled, skating on the sidewalk, bicycling to school, listening to the Beatles, marching in the band. Suddenly, in 1967, this bucolic peace was shattered by a new element. My father heard from friends about Australia, its peace and safety and opportunity, and decided to emigrate—and within months, my twelve-year-old self walked with my family across a gangplank onto a white ship that would take us across the Pacific, over the equator and two tropics, to another life. Caught up in a maelstrom of the new and different, I eventually settled, like a dust speck when the wind dies, and found myself sitting in a high school classroom, wearing a uniform that included a hat and gloves, and tracing for the first time the shapes of characters in a Japanese writing book designed for first-graders. In my somewhat solitary life, two things mattered—Japanese and music. In 1972 I graduated from high school and took a year off to travel to London on a music scholarship. For a time, the fate that was to lead me to Japan wavered and blurred, as I contemplated a career as a professional musician.

Meanwhile, far to the north, a boy was growing up in Japan. Born in that same year of 1955, Toshiro was surrounded by rice fields, summer insect noise, dirt roads, and adults who were starting to breathe again after enduring the long nightmare of the war. Quiet, studious, a bit quirky, a bit timid, reaching the end of high school and successfully navigating "examination hell", he chose a university in Kyoto and found a room in a boarding house with several other boys.

Back in Australia, my boyfriend of that time convinced me, with many arguments, not to go away to study music, but to stay with him and attend the same university. He must have regarded it as quite a coup when I agreed, but my choice of a major was to drive a wedge between us. It was Asian Studies, and especially Japanese, that nudged me, gently at first, away from him and toward my life in Japan. I spent a life-changing six months in Tokyo with a homestay family in 1976, and upon my graduation, I applied for a government scholarship and came to Kyoto for further study in 1978.

The boy who would become my husband made a fascinating friend at his boarding house—a friend who had just returned from a trip to Australia. The young Toshiro, fired with passion for a strange land, dared to travel there alone in 1976, spending forty days almost entirely unable to speak or understand the language, poring over maps, riding trains, and having his entire mind-set transformed. Back in Japan, he immediately joined a friendship organization called the Kobe Japan-Australia Society. One day, the secretary contacted him. She had heard from a teacher friend in Australia that someone was coming to study in Kyoto, and gave him the details (except for the fact that that someone was a girl). The whirlpools of fate were circling, subtly but inexorably moving these two people closer together.

One evening in the spring of 1978, after only six weeks in Kyoto, I answered the door of my student house, and standing there was my future husband. A few days later, we went together to a Japan-Australia Society outing; soon we were dating—both of us fascinated by the tales of each other's country, as well as by the dear uniqueness of each other's self. That summer, when he took me to his country house, I knew the direction my life would take. Within four years we were married; within ten years we had "a family of our own".

In our modern world, there are many ways to experience life, and human beings are much more free to choose a life direction than at other times in history. Having a family is now only one of numerous paths, and may seem, to some, to be a rather mundane and thoughtless one. In our case, our marriage was lifted out of banality by our fascination with all the differences that gave a special flavor to our relationship. I'm proud of what we have made—a family whose bonds are forged not only of commitment, but also of tolerance, interest, respect, and will. Oh, and love, of course.

For the Boys

I grew up in a house of women. My father, a man's man who made a lot of noise in the garage with his power tools and loved his beer and cigarettes, was somewhat uncomfortable and lonely surrounded by a wife and three daughters. He was of the old school—man at work, woman at home—but my mother, a high-powered lady who had once worked at the United Nations, was having none of it. Perhaps she felt the groundswell of Women's Liberation just over the horizon; she was inclined to look down on my father, and on men in general, and her girls followed her example. I realize now that my father had a hard time, and I'm sorry that he had to endure my teenage-daughter angst. I think my dad was overpowered by his own family and by the onward rush of social change. In fact, this was a social phenomenon of the mid-20th century: the disenfranchisement of the father.

When I came to live in Japan, it was like entering a time capsule of earlier sexual mores. At first glance, all the men seemed to be very much on their dignity, and all the women seemed to be practicing self-effacement. (My dad would have fit right in.) Coming from my upbringing, I felt a certain amount of outrage at what I saw as the unearned power of men in Japanese society, and everyone's bland acceptance of this. My unruly tongue got me in trouble more than once at family gatherings, and my mother-in-law despaired of ever getting me to be modest and demure, to let go of (or at least hide) my anger.

These days, the fires of my indignation seem to have burned out. Though the complacency of my male in-laws and the "good old boys" of the village still irritates me sometimes, I can usually maintain my equanimity and sense of humor in my dealings with them. Of course, I think it's a terrible shame that, even in this day and age, many brilliant and talented Japanese women are stuck in the shadow of men, and I think the society would be much improved if the voice of women were heard more. But I don't feel much frustration in my own life from this quarter.

What changed? Well, I got some precious experience in getting to know and love some men of my own. First, I became accustomed to the male energy of my husband, who has been not only a lover, but also a best friend and brother to me. The universal qualities of men—the single-mindedness, the problem-solving, the concentration, the great sense of direction, the assumption of manly responsibilities around the house (trash-burning, pipe-fixing, roof-repairing)—these were probably qualities of my own dad as well, but I never noticed them as positive, because we girls were too busy denigrating them. When they were presented to me in the person of this man I loved, however, I found I loved them too (most of the time).

Then, as if the Universe were determined to balance my early, overly feminine influences, I had two sons. At first I was full of consternation—with no brothers, what did I know about boys?—but I very soon began to enjoy this novel experience. Bringing up boys—the snips and snails and puppy-dog tails—was really fun. Because I had enjoyed some boys' play as a child, collecting rocks, hammering nails, climbing trees, shooting basketball hoops, I could understand the things my own boys liked to do. And it was a relief not to worry about girly things like hairstyles, underwear showing, makeup, etc., none of which I had enjoyed myself as a young girl. Best of all, I received a wholehearted, uncritical love from my sons that I probably wouldn't have had from daughters (I never could have been fashionable enough or appropriate enough in this society for them).

So I'm happy with my boys. My husband is in many ways a quintessential man—an engineer, a handyman, and a number-cruncher extraordinaire. (I can hardly believe some of the things he habitually counts!) He loves maps and train timetables, and constantly dreams about traveling to new places. He's utterly reliable about fixing, or at least trying to fix, things around the house, and his protective concern for me surrounds me like a warm blanket. My elder son, Goki, is a straight arrow—serious and solemn, with a huge sense of responsibility that he seems to obey almost in spite of himself. He has a quirky funny side, though, a lot like his dad, and loves to spend time with his many friends. He looks forward with great joy to being a father and a family man. What a contrast to my younger son, Yuki, a maverick who relishes challenges "because they're there", a one-track-mind perfectionist, a fierce competitor, a stylish, off-the-wall, cool guy who would rather be rich than married. My boys. All so different, all so male.

I even have male cats—four of them. What can I say? I'm hooked.

A family is a microcosm of society. In our family, Japanese society is represented by the boys. All of them went through Japanese school and university, and they are all "out there" dealing with it, swimming in it, every day—they know what to do. My own contribution is Western, though that may be not the best word to describe an energy filtered through a lens now decades old, and influenced by Japan in its turn as well as by my own growth and insights. When the boys come home, beyond the front door is a world we have all made together. It's a comfortable and relaxed one. Each of us speaks whatever language happens to come out of our mouths, peppered with many private family jokes and references. Since we are all busy, our time together is precious, and seldom wasted on things like TV—we have evolved a lot of hilarious games and fun activities, punctuated by serious talks in which the kids actually want to know what Mom and Dad think about things, if you can imagine. And if there's a bit more "guy stuff" than average, like sports talk, cast-off socks on the floor, empty chip bags sitting around for days, and sudden forays in the car to the batting center or the liquor store, I'm OK with that. The Boys—God bless 'em.

The Treasure Chest

See the color insert for the photographs mentioned here.

An old black lacquer trunk, about the size of an army foot locker, slumbers in the dusty darkness of one of our storehouses. It's heavy. Inside, glowing with their own black-light power, are photographs of the family that go back four generations. The worn cardboard covers of navy blue, lilac and grey, with the delicately embossed logos of long-ago photographic studios, and the fragile inner tissue paper, protect the sepia images of my husband's ancestors. Seated on cushions or ornamental chairs, they pose against old-fashioned, stagey backdrops, their faces sober, always gazing slightly off-camera, full of shy pride and deep endurance.

There are other photos, too: snapshots only marginally less formal—still, no one is smiling—and showing, in the background, beams and doorways and gateposts that I recognize. Yes, this was taken in the back garden; and this one, on the veranda outside that room. If the people in the photos were to revisit the house today, they would still be able to find their way around after eighty years.

To look at these pictures properly, I need to refer to the family tree of the Otowa family. This reveals a highly complex tapestry of familial *leger-de-main*. In response to the need to preserve the various branches of the family, as symbolized by the actual physical houses (three in the village at the turn of the twentieth century), couples were created and children shifted around. Families with many children would give one away to a childless relative, and families with daughters would adopt a husband for one of them, to take on the family name and responsibilities.

Here in this photo (Figure 7) are my husband's great-grandparents, Kiichiro and his wife Tomi, seated in our front garden, framed by the delicate mauve lilies that still bloom there every summer. A relatively casual photo; after all, this is their own house. The time was probably the early 1920s. These two, who had no children of their own, adopted their nephew Kisoji as their son, and married him to a distant relative, O-sue, from a different family branch. Meanwhile, O-sue's sister, O-yoshi, was married to another adopted son in order to resurrect the third branch. The two sisters ended up living next door to each other. O-yoshi in the eastern house had five children, while O-sue in the western house (my present house) had none. In these two photos, the young people appear—Kisoji (Figure 8), in 1914, his strong, rugged features offset by a delicate sprig of plum blossom; and the sisters (Figure 9), framing their mother Ima, with a rather strange-looking artificial dog in the corner of the picture. O-yoshi looks pregnant.

This (Figure 10) is a photo of the two sisters, with O-yoshi's five children. In the photo, O-sue holds the youngest daughter—the little girl who grew up to be my mother-in-law. The year is 1935. O-yoshi was very ill when she had her caboose child, Misae, in 1932. It was decided that the baby would be given to the childless couple next door. Thus Misae became an only child, but with four siblings living right next door, attending the same school, playing together every day. From the time I met her, I noticed that my mother-in-law seemed to be simultaneously worried about the opinions of people around her and flouting them to do what she wanted. (For example, she was proud to stand out as having a foreigner for a daughter-in-law, but she also wanted me to be a model Japanese wife.) She must have had "rejection issues" in modern parlance. It's hard to think about her and all those other children, torn from their own parents and placed in other homes to satisfy the implacable requirements of society and tradition. It's hard to think of the psychological wounds they must have carried. No wonder the faces in the photographs are full of a stoic resignation.

Little Misae found herself sharing the new house with another person as well—a young man named Shinzaburo Takahashi, from distant Moriyama on Lake Biwa, who taught at the local primary school and boarded in Kisoji's house. Misae would customarily go to awaken "Teacher" each morning. Soon enough, like so many men, Shinzaburo disappeared into the maw of imperialism and World War II. He remained a teacher, not a combatant, teaching Japanese in the schools of the new colony of Manchuria. Just before the war ended, the luckless Shinzaburo was captured by the Russians and sent to the coal mines near Tomsk in Siberia. There he remained for three years under horrible conditions, watching most of his companions die before eventually making his way back to Japan in 1948. He returned to Otowa, trying to pick up the threads of his previously peaceful life, became the husband of Misae (now seventeen years old), and took the family name as his own. Here's their wedding picture from the following year (Figure 12)—he, the scars of recent hardships subtly evident in his gaze; she, the proud daughter of an ancient line. I bet she was a handful for this man sixteen years her senior.

In time, these people, my husband's parents, had four children of their own. Here is the family on a visit to Nara, circa 1962 (Figure 13). My husband Toshiro, the third child and the first boy to be born into the house in a century, was taken to the shrine for his first ceremony by O-yoshi, his great-aunt and biological grandmother (O-sue having since died). Here they are in this 1955 photograph (Figure 14). The age of camera ownership and individual snapshots was beginning, so from here on, there are many more pictures in the collection, and even color is gradually starting to creep in. The faces are more relaxed, Western clothes gradually edge out kimono; there are more toys and more food and more trips and get-togethers. The sepia atmosphere of hard-lived lives has drained away. From here on, the Otowa family, along with the rest of Japan, began to enter the modern age. Yet I can still sense, as I walk through my house, the sturdy pride of those who have gone before, and I know what was important to them, and I want to pass it on. The black lacquer trunk will stay in its place, waiting to reveal its treasures to the next generation of Otowa.

The Vegetable Patch

One of my best friends in the village is an old lady I'll call Obachan (Auntie). She's eighty if a day, small and wiry, with a frizz of pepper-and-salt hair, a few crooked teeth, and shrewd, merry eyes. Her voice is loud and her movements are definite. Like many old ladies around here, she has effectively retired from the group of women who are required to efface themselves modestly. She's really more like a man.

Obachan is one of a handful of old ladies in the village who battle their various infirmities to work their vegetable patches. Some of them send produce to far-flung family members or sell it at the local farmers' markets; but mostly, it's a way to maintain their view of themselves as productive human beings. Increasingly, their efforts are ignored by daughters-in-law who prefer supermarket veggies that are uniform in size and don't have dirt still sticking to them; but these old aunties persevere, because they are of that thrifty old school that can't stand to see a perfectly good piece of land "going to waste". Another good motivation, of course, is that the vegetable patch is where they can meet with each other regularly and have a good chat.

Obachan is a welcome and important part of my life. She comes to help me with my endless weeding chores or to collect garden trash after the tree-trimmers have finished in the garden. While she works, she talks. I can ask her anything, and she's not shy about replying. From her I learned such village lore as why the owner of the local grocery store committed suicide (an incurable illness), and why the middle-aged, unmarried son of the roofer torched his dad's truck in the middle of the night ("He's not right in the head"). From her I learned the meaning of my latest dream about my mother-in-law, and the preferred method of making certain pickles. Obachan is a perfect mine of information on just about any subject related to everyday life in the village. She's full of judgments, but somehow I don't feel any malice emanating from her. It's just that she has definite opinions and isn't afraid to voice them. I'm glad that her opinion of me is good.

Actually, I'm lucky to have the goodwill of many old village ladies. This came about partly because my own mother-in-law, who was relatively young but full of family pride, took my wifely education very seriously. She tutored me rigorously in village etiquette; her contemporaries saw her efforts and also mine, and approved. From what my mother-in-law told them (she never belittled me in public), as far as they could see, I was an ideal daughter-in-law—easy to mold since I knew nothing, and also polite, tractable and obedient. (Ha!) Of course, the extra cachet of being a *gaijin* (foreigner, outsider) upped the stakes in the endurance department, for both my mother-in-law and me. Commiseration is one of the main oils that grease the wheels in Japanese society, and tales of hardship and woe, which in the West would elicit comments like "Why do you put up with that?" receive the acclamation *"Taihen desu ne"* (That's a lot to bear). The Obachans know I've been through the wringer. Also, by great good fortune, I have a love of gardening, and feel deep satisfaction in growing my own vegetables, however haphazardly. The vegetable patch itself provides an inexhaustible fund of conversation, and gives the aunties a chance to pass on knowledge that their own daughters-in-law mostly aren't interested in. This is another point in my favor.

These old aunties have seen a lot in their day—war, depression, upheaval, shortages, and modernization. Perhaps most poignantly, they have seen society itself shift paradigms, so that they lost out twice: when they were young, age was respected and youth wasn't important; now that they are old, age is pushed aside in favor of the young. The contributions of aged people to the community—wisdom, maturity, experience, and calm—are not valued as they used to be. With this shift has come a change in their status within their families. As young wives themselves, they probably had to endure harsh demands and scolding from older women, but now they find themselves tiptoeing around, trying to stay in the family's good graces. They fear being consigned to the old-age home; they fear being "a bother" when they get ill; and they fear not being remembered with respect and affection after they are

gone. Sometimes I dare to imagine they are happy that a (slightly) younger person like me should enjoy a chat with them and ask their advice.

In general, the people in the village treat me with circumspection after these few decades. They know me; they see me on the street and we exchange greetings. We may be in the same volunteer group, or share communal tasks such as cleanup time at the shrine, but most of their social life is opaque to me. I don't know enough to be a good gossiper, and that means I'm almost entirely oblivious to any gossip about me. I pull my weight in village tasks, and beyond that, I think, for most of them I'm just part of the landscape. The men don't really see women anyway. The women my age have shared children's upbringing, school, and PTA with me; but because of my relatively old-fashioned wifely apprenticeship, I suspect I have been "thrown up to them" by their own mothers-in-law ("If Rebecca-san can do it, why can't you?") which probably doesn't endear them to me. To most of the children, I'm just a familiar oddity. The Obachans are the ones I can really relate to. The vegetable patch sure will be lonely when they are gone.

A Summer Dance

There's one night in August that I always look forward to—the night of the *Bon-Odori*, the summer dance honoring the spirits of the dead who have returned briefly to earth for the *O-Bon* festival. A mini-carnival is set up in front of the village hall, with the *yagura*, a kind of wooden tower, erected for the musicians in the center, and food and game stalls around the edges of the space. From late afternoon, the shrill sound of the music calls the whole village to come and enjoy the welcome cool breezes and the good cheer of neighbors and relatives.

A group of five musicians, dressed in identical cotton *yukata* (summer kimono) of a design so traditional it looks modern, have been hired for the evening. Three rotate on drum, clanging bell, and song, with two resting. The lilting words, all on four notes, are laced with local references and improvisation. The musicians sing and beat with the skill of long practice; the ones at rest stretch their arms along the yagura struts and gaze out over the crowd.

Red and white stripes, the symbol of group celebration, wind around the yagura poles terminating in the wooden roof strung with lanterns that glow and sway. Glaring lights mounted on poles illuminate the scene from some angles, but the dancers are constantly moving in and out of shadows, including the deep shadow of the central platform itself.

They all dance their own way and they do it every year. Circling the yagura, the dancers move to the right, stop and clap, move to the right, stop and clap, on a rhythm of six beats, each repetition ending on a different beat of the song. All the old people and most of the younger people take a turn. Small children run back and forth through the circle. Teenagers stand well away from the action; seeming to observe the dance, they are actually directing laser-like glances at the group of opposite-sex kids on the other side of the circle.

An old man dancing—his spare, jerky movements somehow convey an immense zest for life and tell the story of decades of dancing through good times and bad.

Fitting myself into the groove of the dance form, the music is like the needle that hits the groove and calls up the gestures, the stepping and clapping, from the memory of last summer. All are in the groove, dancers and musicians—a totality of movement, sight and sound.

Yagura *platform, with musicians performing at* Bon-Odori

Around the fringe of the circle are the food and game stalls—each with a tank-top-clad man lounging on a folding chair, a couple of gazing children, and people striding up self-consciously to avail themselves of the wares. There are mothers squatting to stuff chopstickfuls of fried noodles into their children's mouths, genial neighbors laughing over cans of beer, young couples showing off their new babies, fiftyish aunties dressed up as hula dancers, toddlers in frothy cotton kimonos watching the scene all solemn and big-eyed, elder brothers edging toward legal drinking age sneaking beers in the shadows, and committee members standing importantly with folded arms or striding off in one direction or another.

Over it all, the vibrant music, the rubbery stretching and shrinking of the song proceed to the punctuating boom and click of the drum and the dinging of the bell and the shuffling and claps of the dancers and the hiss of the generator.

I've danced here almost every summer of my married life. I've danced in yukata and fancy dress, with my husband and my in-laws, with neighbors I didn't like at all, and with friends I was glad to see. I've taught the dance to my sons when they could barely walk, and shared a beer with them when they towered over me. But mostly I've fitted myself into that groove and danced the Bon-Odori, making circuit after circuit, because this is one of the times when I can hold close to my heart the elusive certainty that I too am part of this place.

Off and Running

O ctober has come to our town. White plastic tents emblazoned with village names are being dragged out of storage, mysterious cardboard constructions crowd the lobbies of the village meeting halls, and committee members rush around or stand scrutinizing the weather with worried, important faces. Everyone is getting ready for the annual Municipal Athletic Meet.

This meet, in which eight or so local areas come together in competition, was instituted around the time my husband was born. In those days, it was considered an honor to compete for one's village; but now it's become more of a time for people from the various villages to spend a day in the sunshine (they hope), gossiping and catching up with long-time-no-see relatives and old school chums. There's a cheerful holiday mood, but running through it all like a tightly strung cord is Organization. As a counterpoint to all the gabbing and conviviality, the actual athletic events are being carried out with teeth-gritting determination by both the competitors and the organizers.

The athletes, our neighbors, have been painstakingly persuaded to attend and assigned their places in the events weeks ago. Men and women, youngsters and oldsters, their names are listed on huge posters on display at each village tent. Lined up on the periphery of the primary school sports ground, these tents are Home Base, both for the competitors, who report here to pick up the numbered cloth vests which signify their participation, and also for the spectators (mostly competitors between events). Here everyone takes up a position according to a hierarchy that is unwritten but strictly observed. In the very front of the shaded area, the female Elders of the Village kneel on cushions, with their devoted daughters-in-law and adoring but squirmy grandchildren just behind them. As for the men, they don't sit on cushions in the shade—that would be too wussy. They prefer to hang around the folding chairs at the back, within a long arm's reach of the sake bottle, or to stand with folded arms watching the action from under their baseball caps. Regular Mom-types are a floating population and may be seen everywhere, chatting, tending to children, tying shoelaces, arranging elaborate lunch boxes, and subtly taking each other's measure—in fashion, weight, demeanor, and children's behavior. Kids dash around everywhere, but the teenagers keep their distance and spend the day nonchalantly bragging to each other under the soccer net.

The glaring white sand burns the bottoms of the eyes, and the limpid blue of the sky relieves them. In between, tiny figures run, jump, fall down, pull on ropes, dash busily about, or stand self-consciously. Bursts of applause greet the winners, but the loudest cheering is reserved for the "trier" who finishes the race—last—with a scraped knee or a twisted ankle. The races are measured and points awarded, until finally the Grand Prize Winner emerges, to be presented (amid suitable pomp) with the coveted Loving Cup Trophy and Bunches of Flags. It's considered quite all right for ordinary participants to sneak away during the closing remarks, but the faithful committee members remain till the bitter end, folding tents, separating trash, winding up ropes. They are exhausted, but in their hearts they cherish a comforting ember of light: "It will be someone else's turn next year."

The Japanese are very good at exertion in group situations. It seems that the group plays the role of conscience in determining how to behave, and social judgment, called *seken no me* (the Eye of the World), determines the degree of each person's exertion before, during, and after the activity. Of course, offices that are passed around the neighborhood from year to year—like the Athletic Meet committee—are loaded with social nuance. You can't let the side down. Even if you have a very good reason, you will be subtly made to feel guilty if you don't take your turn. This is why established institutions, like the Athletic Meet, are extremely difficult to change or abolish. To refuse to accept the torch passed on from Those Who Have Gone Before is to negate all their efforts.

So the grand old tradition will persist for another year, even though the number of participants is falling steadily. And on the field, the figures with whistles and clipboards will have different faces, but will otherwise display their exertion in exactly the same way to the watching neighbors whose turn it isn't. The social conscience will be salved, and group influence—which so far is still winning out over individual desire—will prevail.

The glad hand makes the rounds
And the Eye of the World is watching.

A Village Gathering

Social groups in our village cut in many different directions. First, there are the *tonari-gumi* ("next door groups") or blocks of families, whose main functions are dispersion of information, collection of fees, and funeral support. Overlapping these are the Women's Association, the Senior Citizen's Association, the parishes of the three temples, and other smaller groups affiliated with various shrines and Shinto deities. One example of this last is the Atago-ko, associated with Atago shrine in Kyoto, which my family has belonged to for a couple of hundred years. The eight families in the group take turns each January to provide a dinner for everyone, and to make a pilgrimage to the shrine on behalf of the group. This year it's our turn, and on the appointed day, the twenty-third day of the first month, or 1-2-3, we held the dinner at our house.

In most of these traditional neighborhood events, there has been a gradual simplification, and now most of the dinner is not prepared by the family, but ordered in from the local shop. The hosts are expected to provide only rice, soup, sweets and drinks, and of course the Shinto purification materials including *sakaki* leaves, rice grains, and sake.

After the guests arrive, they are greeted by the hosts, and make their obeisance to the shrine deity (represented by a hanging scroll), each taking a few grains of rice on a leaf, conveying it to their mouths, and sipping the sacred sake. Then the box lunches are opened, the drink starts to flow, and the party warms up. My husband sits with the guests and keeps an eye on things, while I stay in the kitchen, heating the rice wine in the little ceramic bottles. I serve sake, collect empty bottles, provide tea for the inevitable non-drinking woman, and once in a while, sit down and have a drink and a chat with the guests myself. (I carry my own wee sake cup in my pocket.)

The conversation ranges over such topics as this year's cold weather compared to last year's, old-time memories of the village ("there used to be so many shops"), school and childhood recollections, the relative merits of different kinds of sake, the occasional wartime reminiscence. One member, a carpenter, admiringly points out features of a hand-made antique bureau in the room. Once in a while a mild tinge of naughtiness colors the conversation—as when the talk turns to a local recreational table tennis club, triggering good-natured word play and laughter about balls.

Sitting in the kitchen, with half an ear on the talk and half an eye on my book, I reflect that for women anyway, the role of hostess is more comfortable than that of guest. Sure it's bothersome for the hostess to set things up and then run around serving everyone, but if she were a guest, she would have to sit cramped on the floor, stifling yawns as the evening goes on and waiting for someone to notice that she needs more tea (no one pours his own drinks at social gatherings).

Japanese people generally do not drink alcohol with rice at these formal dinners, so one of the host's jobs is to gauge when everyone has "had enough" and the last phase, with soup, rice, tea, and pickles, can begin (often two or three hours after the meal has commenced). After that, there must be an indefinite period of conversation while the subliminal psychic signals, or belly-to-belly communication, filter through the group. No one leaves early, but when one person starts to make "Well, it's getting

Hanging scroll representing the deity of Atago Shrine

late" noises, the party is over in a twinkling. Hastily wrapping up their take-home fruit and sweets, they make a rush for the line of shoes in the entrance-way, exchanging bows with the hosts before stepping, gloved, bundled and red-cheeked, out into the cold night.

Many of these traditional meeting groups are falling victim to modern indifference or lack of time; but as I gather up dishes and stack cushions and wipe tables, I reflect that everyone enjoyed themselves tonight. There was a good mix of people—middle-aged and elderly, extroverts and introverts, beer drinkers and sake drinkers, men and women—most of whom have known each other since they were children. Although there would undoubtedly be sighs of relief on the part of the hosts, I think there would also be a feeling of sadness if the Atago-ko were to go the way of the other lamented Things of the Good Old Days.

The Spirit of the House

Small triangular kamidana
shelf near the kitchen

Stained glass window in entryway, installed in 2007

The House Speaks

The stoves have been turned off, and I feel the heat gradually leave me as the New One's footsteps die away down the stone path. The clock ticks softly; there is no other sound but the occasional whisper of cats settling on the chairs or moving sinuously through the gaps in the sliding doors. I am without human occupation this day. It is a perfect time to feel my own feelings and think my own thoughts.

The New One is the Heir's wife, the present custodian. I call her the New One because she has a certain kind of energy that I have never felt before, in all the generations of humans I have sheltered. She often goes out, but she almost always returns the same day. Even when she is gone, I can feel her bond, the strength of her vow. She and the Heir are going to take care of me—they have sworn it—I am safe for another generation.

I am one of the lucky ones. All around me, houses my age or even younger are suffering the pain and indignity of being reduced to a heap of gray wood, splinters of bamboo, plaster dust, and broken tiles. Even the stones which once proudly held up the pillars are dug out of the earth and taken away. In place of the previous old house, the occupants, who are usually the Original

Families (people who belong here, who don't come from outside), put up some kind of new structure—I would hesitate to call it a house—with no verandas, no tatami, no beams, no roof tiles. The wood struts are woefully puny and insubstantial. I know these neighborhood upstarts won't last, not as I have lasted. I miss the old houses. They were my neighbors, my fellows, my friends.

Of course I cannot count the winters that have passed since I began my life. The Heir has tried—he is very interested in numbers—but the blessing papers from the shrine, put into the rafters at the time of my building, are no longer readable. Still, he estimates I have stood considerably more than three hundred winters, and the Original Family has lived under my roof for at least sixteen generations. Let those flimsy, chemical-ridden structures around me try to beat that record!

It's no wonder I have lasted so long, with the good strong materials that went into me. The largest piece of wood in my structure is the huge cross-beam, carved from a single tree trunk, and stretching through living room, kitchen and breezeway. It's about twelve meters long, and has a cross-section of almost forty centimeters, in the new measurement system they use these days. There's an interesting story about this beam. When it was cut from the forest and carried to this site, at a certain point it had to turn a corner in the town, but it was too long—there was no way the humans could make it go around the corner. So they decided to break down the earthen temple wall on the corner to allow the passage of the beam (the wall was later rebuilt with many apologies). They broke a temple wall rather than shorten that beam—I feel very proud when I consider that. It's a sign that my family was real quality.

When I was first built, I took the same form as most houses in this area. There were four rooms arranged in a square, with raised floors (another sign of quality—most homes had mainly dirt floors in those days) surrounded by wooden verandas and an attached, roofed kitchen area. One of the rooms had a fire pit or hearth, and a hole in the roof above (covered, of course), to let the smoke out. My new beams and pillars were painted with *bengara* (a red iron-oxide pigment mixed with charcoal) to make the soft, dark, purplish-brown color that the occupants liked, and to discourage insects. Time after time, I felt the soothing rub of cloth bags filled with rice germ to bring up the shine of my wood, and damp cloths to remove dust. I was like a thoroughbred horse (a very long-lived one!), lovingly cleaned and curried by generations of hands.

Since then, my rooms have increased, and I have had new roofs and new floors. Many members of the Original Family have come and gone. I have been witness to times of pain and grief, and times of happiness and celebration. There were births, marriages, and deaths, all under my roof. I am proud to have sheltered them faithfully, and they in turn have dedicated themselves to my well-being. Now the present occupants are here. The Heir is very proud of me and he has taught his children to be proud too. I think I can feel sure that these children will honor me when their turn comes.

As for the wife, the New One—she comes from so far away I can't even imagine it. She has made some interesting changes: there's a strange kind of colored glass window in the entryway now, and inside, there are some new wood floors, to say nothing of the furniture! Chairs, the like of which I've never seen! Spotlights in the ceiling! Glass tiles in the kitchen roof to let in more light! Her voice is different, and her motions and rhythms are too. But she takes care of me, sweeping and polishing as best she can, and she loves me. I can feel her heart. I know she will stay.

Was that the car door slamming? Were those footsteps on the stones? Ah—you see? Here she is, back from her outing. I will be warm again.

A Family Story

This is a true story that dates back to the very beginnings of the Otowa family.

In the year 1619, when the Tokugawa government had consolidated Japan into one nation and imposed order on the land, a boundary dispute arose between the eastern and western regions of the plain adjoining the Suzuka mountain range, to the east of Otowa village. The dispute concerned the rights to the use of the mountains, whose forests in those days were the principal source of fuel, and charcoal-burning one of the few occupations that brought cash money to the farmers. Many wild provisions—fruits, herbs, mushrooms, and game—were also to be found there.

The dispute could not be resolved, and a certain man, Kakubei, a short-term resident of the western region, suggested that the west challenge the east to a trial by ordeal. This kind of trial had been practiced since the seventh century, but had almost died out by the time the Tokugawa came into power. In the present case, a representative from each faction would take a red-hot iron axe in his hands and carry it to the altar of the shrine. Whichever man succeeded in this task would win the rights to the disputed land for his faction. The trial by ordeal had become so unusual that two government officials were sent to witness it and judge the outcome.

In the preparations for the trial, Kakubei stood as the representative of the western faction, and for the eastern, an elder named Kurazaemon offered to stand. But the western faction objected that Kisuke of Otowa, a local official who had been active in the dispute, was trying to shirk the ordeal. With rumors of cowardice flying, Kisuke took over the task from Kurazaemon in order to uphold the honor of his house. Thus all was decided, and the day of the trial set for the eighteenth day of the ninth month.

Early on that fateful morning, the people assembled in the shrine precincts. One figure waited alone outside the gate. This was Kisuke's mother Umeko, who had put on a white mourning kimono and, with her *naginata* (long sword) upraised, stood ready to strike down her own son if he should return in shame.

The tall cypresses looked down from all around onto the greensward striped with long shadows. The dancers, with their crisp red and white garments and their ceremonial hand bells, performed the purification rites, and the priests and officials waited for the smiths to prepare the fire. Blue-white smoke rose up into the clear crisp autumn air. The iron axes were laid on the fire to heat; the two representatives, dressed in white, stood to attention; the officials rose to give the signal for the trial to begin. A hush fell over the crowd.

At the very last moment, one official suddenly stopped the proceedings and ordered the two men to change places and each to carry the axe prepared for the other. No one knew why this occurred. Perhaps it was an inspiration of the gods. Kakubei, at that instant, was observed to turn very pale. Had he attempted a ruse of some sort, which had backfired? The western faction was known to have skillful ironmongers—perhaps their axe had somehow been tampered with to make the ordeal easier, and perhaps the official had some intuition of this.

The two men stepped forward and received the red-hot iron axes in their hands to walk the short distance to the altar. Kakubei immediately screamed, dropped his burden, and turned to flee, but in vain—he was apprehended, and the following day met his end by execution in the nearby field of Hibarino. Kisuke, meanwhile, in great agony, managed to convey the axe to the altar, and put his blackened and smoking palms together in obeisance. The axe he ended up with may indeed have been illegally manufactured by the western faction to be easier to carry, but that was immaterial. He had won, and the eastern faction had gained the rights to the mountain. Great was the rejoicing in Otowa village that night; and Kisuke sat in the place of honor, his useless hands in his lap while his mother Umeko raised the sake cup to his lips as he was toasted again and again.

As a result of that trial, Kisuke's family was awarded the land on Toyama, a distinctive triangular hill and the tallest peak in the nearby range. To this day the Otowa family celebrates the *Tekka matsuri* (Festival of red-hot iron). The descendants of Kisuke go to that same shrine in the chilly air of an autumn morning and hold a ceremony to commemorate that brave deed of long ago. In the present generation of our family, there is another reason to remember this story: the day of the festival was chosen as our wedding day.

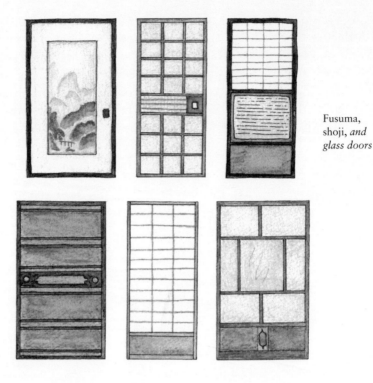

Fusuma,
shoji, *and*
glass doors

Changing the Doors

Everyone knows that a wall is an immovable barrier which keeps things and people in or out, and that a door is a conduit or portal where movement from one space to another is either permitted or restricted. A wall never becomes a door, or a door a wall. They are separate entities with contradictory functions. These are the semantic imperatives that I absorbed in my childhood world of American suburbia.

Coming to Japan, in many ways, forced me to notice the arbitrary nature of words in deciding How Things Are. My house now is just as much of an entity as my childhood ranch-style four-bedroom bungalow was, yet the paradigms, the assumptions of psychological priorities, are completely different. The interior "walls" consist entirely of sliding doors, in sets of four, which may be opened at any point or even removed bodily to suit the immediate functions of the rooms themselves. In the designs of these doors I can read the interior decorating tastes of succeeding generations of residents: they are fashioned of wood, paper, glass, and reeds, in different combinations, with everything from simple lattice-work to busy, over-conceived geometrical shapes. Whatever their appearance, however, their basic structure is the same—they have only the most rudimentary handles, and of course, no locks. Are they doors at all, in the sense I have always understood the word? In conjunction with the all-purpose nature of most rooms and their lack of furniture or impedimenta, the distinction between door and wall is, for the most part, nonexistent. It's a freestyle way of living that I've come to like, the big clean spaces, floored with tatami that is easy on the feet, ceilinged with remote dark wood slats, and in between, these doors, properly called *tategu* ("standing things").

The material of the doors varies with the seasons. In June, the dark, solid winter doors are exchanged for lighter ones made of reeds that allow the free flow of cooling breezes. Oh, but the word "exchanged" cloaks a long procedure—hauling the summer doors out of the storehouse where they are kept; wiping them down; removing the winter doors and carrying them to the storehouse; and finally puzzling out which summer door goes where. (They all look the same, but are marked on the top edge with cryptic directions such as "Outer East", which if ignored will result in misaligned and emphatically non-sliding doors.) A complete *koromogae* (door-changing) entails the shifting of thirty-four units of tategu. But troublesome though it is, this exchange of doors, whether in spring or fall, gives the house a feeling of freshness, and oneness with the season, that is hard to achieve in many Western houses.

The most common interior doors are *shoji* and *fusuma*. Both are wood frames with paper glued on. Again, this sounds simple, but there is a wealth of activity hidden in that word "glued". Shoji paper is white and relatively flimsy, but surprisingly efficient as a heat insulator. It tears easily, and a torn shoji door is like a chipped cup—the eye is inevitably drawn to the imperfection. Also, the pristine whiteness of the paper tends to grow dull with the passage of time, so that shoji must be renewed when necessary in a process of washing and drying the frames, and measuring, cutting, and gluing the paper. The glue is semitransparent mucilage traditionally made from rice. Fusuma are double-sided, opaque doors made of heavier paper which is often decorated with ink paintings or calligraphy. But it's still paper, it can still be damaged by a careless broomstick or a skittish cat, and will require repair of a more complicated kind.

Most other doors in the house are made of wood, sometimes with frosted glass inserts, and their maintenance is a simple matter of dusting. Simple? Dusting? Again, these are misleading words. The average door has between ten and thirty separate and distinct horizontal ledges, each of which must be wiped with a damp cloth wrapped around a finger. The dark wood shows dust easily, both dust that blows in from outside and dust that filters down from the centuries-old ceiling. It's a never-ending task, or perhaps it just seems never-ending, when fingers grow numb and puckered in the chill of the winter "big cleaning" time.

Writing this, and thinking about the doors in my home, it strikes me how full of nuance, how nebulous in meaning, how bound by culture, each word in a language is. For me, a closed door implies privacy; but there is no indigenous word in Japanese for "privacy", and when I consider what doors, walls, and rooms mean in this culture, I understand why. Of course, understanding is one thing, and getting used to it was quite another; but the semantic adventure has softened the psychological stress. Throwing meaning to the winds— rediscovering every day that physical objects are no more and no less than the definitions we give them—is an experience both unnerving and liberating. And no matter how long I live here, I probably won't come to the end of it.

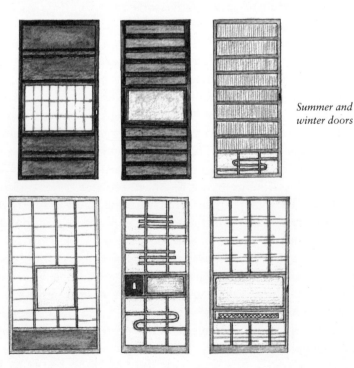

Summer and winter doors

*Five-yen coin, showing
ripe heads of rice*

The Harvest

September is the month that sees the achingly green, soft carpet of the rice fields gradually assume a tawny hue, as the grain heads appear and bend down in the graceful and replete way of grasses. Under the infinitely pure and deep autumn sky, the red combine harvesters chug their way around the fields, devouring the rows of plants on one end and producing neat bags of rice on the other. The straw floats down to the muddy ground in a golden coverlet, between the rows of stubble. Both straw and stubble will later be burnt off to provide soil nutrients for next year.

The colors of autumn in our countryside are the chartreuse of ripe fields, the rich ochre of the stubble, and the brilliant scarlet of the harvesters, which is echoed in the crimson clumps of *higan-bana* ("equinox flower" or spider lily), a wildflower that stands along the grass verges only at this time of year. The sounds of autumn are the drone of harvesters and of the rice-drying machines in farm sheds by day, and the tired-sounding crickets grinding out their endless songs by night. The scents are the sour reek of fallen persimmons, the warm dusty miasma of straw and rice husks, and the sharp tang of the blue-smoke burning stubble.

When we were first married, we still grew rice in our family fields. I have spent hours with bent back, collecting and tying straw, or standing in the mind-numbing cacophony of our antiquated machines, like Tess of the D'Urbervilles, feeding in the bundles of rice until it grew too dark to see. Finally the task got to be too much for us, and for our machines. Now we depend on generous neighbors to work our land.

In these sweet mild days of September, the rice-drying machine next door rattles and blows all day, sending forth a pattering shower of rice husks that pile up in a golden mountain as high as my head. These husks are valuable in the garden as mulch and for aerating the soil. Yesterday I went over to collect rice husks in big cloth bags—a year's supply. Standing ankle-deep in the soft, powdery, itchy stuff, showered by more husks as they came flying out of the drying shed, I felt as though I were bathing in it. Uncomfortable, yes, but I also felt strangely contented and even wealthy. Each husk represented a rice grain; some of them would, at some time during the next year, find their way to our table.

This feeling of contentment and wealth has plenty of historic precedent in Japan. In the old days, rice was for the rich, and the peasants paid their taxes in rice. Subsisting on buckwheat, potatoes, and even acorn flour, they regarded the overlords, with their storehouses stacked with the barrel-shaped straw bales of rice, almost as beings from another world. The *koban* (gold pieces) used as currency were shaped like rice bales. Even today, the pictur-

esque gold-colored five-yen coin is decorated with heavy heads of rice curving around the hole in the middle. The name of this coin, *"go-en"*, means "fortune" as well as "five yen", and it is frequently used in offerings.

My husband's ancestors were farmers for many generations. This was a much respected social category in the feudal period, second only to the samurai, and this can be seen in the size and position of the house and the number of storehouses on the property. Today, of course, for almost all Japanese, rice comes from the local supermarket, but in our family we still feel privileged to eat rice that has been grown in our own fields, within sight of our front door.

> *Our own house*
> *Our own land*
> *Our own food*
> *Is this not wealth?*
> *Let us give thanks for another harvest.*

Shoki, *a protective deity, on a hanging scroll in the* tokonoma

Household Gods

I live in an old house. Every day, waking and sleeping, I live with its history; I walk through memories and sit down with unseen presences. Some of these presences are the twenty or so generations' worth of past occupants, and some are the household gods. I'd like to introduce them, but before I do, I'd better define some terms.

For most Japanese people, the word "god" does not have the meaning we ascribe to it in Western countries. They do not conceive of one all-powerful deity central to the religious experience, who is concerned with individual human souls; conversely, they do not see themselves as bound in a sacred covenant to believe in or obey a deity on pain of eternal damnation. Rather, the word *kami* (god) denotes an entity or spirit, usually inherent in a particular natural place, such as a great tree, mountain, crag, or waterfall. It is a kind of aura surrounding the place, an energy which evokes awe and veneration.

The indigenous religion of Shinto is a way of approaching the holiness of natural phenomena. The supplicant must first be purified, and he then calls forth the kami by clapping, and on special occasions, dancing, offering food and wine, and verbal invocation. Because of the emphasis on purification, Shinto is central in ceremonies of beginning: the New Year, weddings, childbirth, and also events such as building construction. Also, the plurality and variety of kami make Shinto an all-purpose blessing religion, answering every human entreaty from success in examinations to protection from accident, and expressing human gratitude in ceremonies for disposal of used fishing gear, calligraphy brushes, sewing needles, and the like. It is also the religion of planting and harvest, and its shrines are the venues for the attendant seasonal festivals.

Around the seventh century, Buddhism was brought from China to Japan as part of a broad wave of cultural assimilation. More complex and consciously otherworldly than Shinto, Buddhism emphasized the spirit over the body, and believed that the misery of life—the wheel of reincarnation—was to be escaped through spiritual practices leading to enlightenment. As their elements tangled and mixed over the centuries, Buddhism and Shinto became the two pillars of organized religion in Japan, with exactly complementary social functions—Shinto handled matters of life, and Buddhism, those of death.

Neither of these religions contains any hint of celestial judgment, mercy, reward, or punishment, as these are known in the West (although based on the cause-and-effect mechanism of karma, Buddhists have invented some spectacular paradises and some terrifying hells). Neither mentions eternity, and neither presupposes any personal emotional connection with a deity involving either love or fear. Instead, religion in Japan is practical, eclectic, broad and functional, a tool for navigating the rapids of human life and for social bonding. Thus, a businessman will go off to the Buddhist funeral of a colleague, and returning home, will sprinkle a small packet of salt, provided at that same funeral, to be purified in the Shinto manner before entering his front door.

This eclecticism is abundantly evident in my home. We have four places which could be described as altars. Foremost is the *butsudan* ("Buddha-cabinet") in the main room, which houses our image of Amida, the deity of the Pure Land sect. The ancestors of the family are also associated with the butsudan (since they are dead, and Buddhism is the religion of death), and it is here that they are venerated during the summer O-Bon festival.

Beside the butsudan is the *tokonoma*, or honorary alcove, a raised dais with various decorations. Here reside the formidable *Shoki* (protective deities), portrayed on a hanging scroll, and the *koma-inu*, a ceramic figure which recalls the Chinese lion-dogs flanking the entrances to shrines. Both these entities are believed to protect the house, and they receive veneration and decorations of candles, o-mochi, and sake at New Year.

The third altar is in the reception room leading from the entrance hall, fastened to a wall so high above my head that I can't place things on it without standing on a chair. This is the *kamidana* or god-shelf, which houses the main

Shinto gods of the household with their offerings. These deities also receive attention mainly at New Year, when the shelf is decorated with fresh leaves of sasaki, the sacred tree of Shinto.

Finally, just outside the kitchen door is a small triangular shelf for the kitchen gods. Dominated in our home by the deity of Atago Shrine, these gods protect us in kitchen tasks, especially those related to fire. The usual decoration is a vase of sasaki.

Even though I was raised a Christian, I am perfectly happy taking care of these altars. The everyday maintenance of placing flowers and leaves is easy and low-key, and there is a pleasant formality in the bowing and clapping at New Year and O-Bon. I like the idea of the unseen entities who share my home. I wish all these household gods well, and I hope they wish me well. The ancestors, in particular, are a palpable presence, embodying the spirit of the house itself. I feel that they watch over us, rejoice and grieve with us, and observe the strength and constancy of our hearts as custodians of the house.

The longer I live here, the more I feel that everything around me is in some measure sacred. How can God, whoever or whatever that is, be present in some things and not in others? And if God is in everything, is God in me as well? The main altar of a Shinto shrine suggests the possibility—the central decoration is a mirror, in which I can see the divine in myself.

Koma-inu *(Chinese lion-dog),
a protective deity*

Incense burning in metal altar incense burner

The Spirits Return

J apan has been generally known as a country of "ancestor worship". This term may evoke gasps of outrage from some religious people, but it is not strictly true. The ancestors are not, in fact, worshipped as gods—but they are revered as awakened beings and protectors of the family. Death seems to confer enlightenment, and the dead are referred to as *hotoke-sama* (Buddhas, or awakened ones). The spirit world sometimes seems very close in Japan, and the dead of our family aren't scary ghosts, but our friends and advisors. We show them our successes and accomplishments—diplomas, wedding photos, and other things may be placed before the altar for a few days. We take our leave of them when we go on a trip, and inform them when we come back. They remain in our thoughts almost as if they themselves are away on an extended trip, and there is even a season when they return for a visit—the O-Bon festival in mid-August.

The visitors from the spirit world arrive on this earthly plane on the evening of August 13th. To welcome them, the family butsudan is decorated with fruit, flowers, incense, and candles. The village priest comes to chant sutras. For the next few days, the ancestral spirits will get special treatment, including their own vegetarian meals served on tiny doll-sized lacquer dishes. Living relatives also gather to exchange family news, and there is a sense of conviviality and completeness. It is the busiest time of year as people make their way back to their childhood homes—freeways are jammed, airplanes and trains are bursting at the seams. The holiday is a kind of combination Thanksgiving, All Souls' Day, and Halloween.

During the visit, we walk up to the family graveyard, which has been cleaned and tidied in preparation. Our graveyard is a quiet bower, a clearing in the grove, with ancient, worn tombstones dotted here and there in the grass. It's also a haven for mosquitoes, so the water pouring, incense lighting, flower arranging, and praying are punctuated by humming and slapping. (At these times, I fervently hope none of our ancestors have been reborn on Earth as mosquitoes.) On the afternoon of August 15th, to the chinging sound of the portable altar bell, families carry the offerings of fruit and flowers from the butsudan down through the bamboo forest to the river bank, arranging them on temporary altars of stones at the water's edge. This is the ritual of seeing off the ancestral spirits as they go away to the Pure Land (the Buddhist Paradise) until next year.

Candlestick in the butsudan

The following week, the children have their own O-Bon festival, setting up shelters at the local roadside shrines consecrated to their patron saint, O-Jizo. In the daytime they play games and eat snacks contributed by neighbors; at night they roam the graveyards and other dark, spooky places, gleefully jumping out at each other in tests of courage.

I don't know the ancestral spirits personally, although some people have told me they feel their presence in various places in the house. Once, alone in the daytime (not at O-Bon), I looked out the window of the living room and saw the forms of two elderly people, dressed in old-fashioned garb, walking along the outside wall of the house, engaged in conversation. I have also occasionally heard footsteps or the sound of doors. I guess in a house of this age, many images and impressions have soaked into the structure over the generations.

Because of the O-Bon Festival, the lush vegetation of summer, the searing heat, and the shrilling of insects are linked in my mind with weathered tombstones and the aroma of incense. It's a contrast with childhood Halloween images of the full moon and chilly grasses of autumn. But in the lunar calendar, August is already the beginning of autumn, so perhaps the two festivals are not so far removed after all. The year has passed its zenith, and ahead are change, decay and death. It's an appropriate time to feel the nearness of spirits.

FIGURE 1 View of the house from the *O-Jizo* shrine on the southwest corner. At the time of original construction, the entire front yard area was built up to level from a steep slope down to the river, and secured with a mortarless stone wall on the south and west sides.

FIGURE 2 The south-facing entrance to the house is approached over a flagstone yard that is as old as the house itself. Flanking the front door is a formal garden with a traditional roofed gate.

FIGURE 3 The main room, or *okunoma*, houses the *butsudan* with Buddha icons and offerings of flowers, incense, fruit, candles and water. Beside it is the *tokonoma* (ceremonial alcove), with its scroll and decorations.

FIGURE 4 Surrounding the older part of the house is a long wooden veranda, shielded from the elements by glass-paneled sliding doors. In summer, these doors are thrown open to catch every breeze, and the verandas, overhung with deep eaves, are a favorite cool spot for snoozing cats.

FIGURE 5 Before New Year, we make *o-mochi* (glutinous rice cakes) in a traditional wooden mortar with a large mallet. Special rice is steamed, and salt added before pounding it until smooth and sticky. Pounding is my son Yuki, and my job is to quickly turn the hot mass with wet hands between blows of the mallet.

FIGURE 6 The boys—Toshiro, Goki, and Yuki—during an excursion to a local aquarium around 1996.

FIGURE 7 Great-grandparents Kiichiro and Tomi, sometime in the 1920's, with the front veranda in the background. Though it is a casual snapshot, Kiichiro holds a fan, which suggests it may have been a family or temple occasion.

FIGURE 8 In this much more formal photograph, Kisoji, the adopted son of Kiichiro and Tomi, poses for his portrait in 1914.

FIGURE 9 O-sue and O-yoshi flank their mother Ima in a formal studio portrait. O-yoshi is probably pregnant with one of her five children.

FIGURE 10 In this family snapshot circa 1935, O-yoshi (right) poses with her family of five near the neighborhood temple. In the center, O-sue holds the caboose child, Misae (my mother-in-law), who had become her adopted daughter.

FIGURE 11 An early snapshot of our front house, probably dating from the 1920s. Although the garden was smaller then, it is still recognizably the same as in Figure 1.

FIGURE 12 Misae Otowa and Shinzaburo Takahashi on their wedding day in 1949. She was only 17, he was in his thirties. It was a marriage arranged by the families, at Shinzaburo's request. Misae must have been a handful for the exhausted veteran of a Siberian prison camp, but he clearly had lost none of his personal pride.

FIGURE 13 Shinzaburo and Misae with their family on an excursion to Nara in the early 1960s. The two little sons, Hidekazu and Toshiro, are flanked by their big sisters, Kiyoko and Michiko.

FIGURE 14 Baby Toshiro, dressed up for his first visit to the local shrine, is proudly held by his biological grandmother, O-yoshi. The year is 1955.

FIGURE 15 In autumn, the communal vegetable fields are redolent of the scents and colors of this most peaceful of seasons.

FIGURE 16 Japanese villages commonly have canals for water management, sometimes centuries old. This little canal flows past our house and then west through the neighboring villages, parallel to the Hino River.

FIGURE 17 Homes are purified for the new year on January 21st by a group of lion dancers who travel to Hino from the Grand Shrine of Ise in neighboring Wakayama Prefecture.

FIGURE 18 The spectacular Hino Festival on May 3 involves a large percentage of the population, especially youths under age 30. Huge floats are trundled up the main street of the town as they have been for centuries, and everyone congregates at *Watamuki* Shrine for a day of ceremonies and fun.

FIGURE 19 Watamuki Shrine, dedicated to the god of Mt. Watamuki (east of Otowa, part of the Suzuka mountain range) was the scene of the *Tekka Saiban*, a trial by ordeal held to settle a land dispute, which Kisuke of Otowa won in 1619.

FIGURE 20 Entrance to *Unko-ji* Temple, a Pure Land Sect temple which has counted our family among its parishioners for several centuries.

FIGURE 21 Our family temple, Unko-ji, is famous for its venerable old azalea bushes, giving it the nickname "*Satsuki-dera*" (Azalea Temple). We are often surprised to find photographs of the temple on calendars depicting scenic Japanese gardens.

FIGURE 22 Another neighborhood temple is *Yosen-ji*, a New Pure Land sect temple which boasts the only bell tower in the village. There is a 400-year-old flowering plum tree in its precincts.

FIGURE 23 I was married to Toshiro Otowa on October 18, 1981. The ceremony was held in our house, in front of the *butsudan*, and afterwards this photo was taken in our front garden. Toshiro wears his grandfather's wedding outfit. My own outfit features the traditional *wataboshi*, or "cotton hat", a type of white veil.

In the Midst of Nature

Seasons

L iving through the seasons of a year in Japan, I get a real physical sense of the Earth's stately progress through the heavens, tethered by the leash of gravity to its god, the sun. The rise and fall of one seasonal feature after another create an endless flow pattern which permeates every corner of consciousness.

The eye is filled with colors—spring with its sweet pastels, summer with its strong primary colors, autumn with its meditative tonality, winter with its monochrome. Into the ear pour the birdsong of spring, the screaming cicada buzz of summer, the meditative chirping of autumn crickets, the eerie silence of winter. Perhaps the most visceral of the senses, taste and smell, provide the deepest links in memory to seasonal phenomena. As time progresses, the taste buds begin to long for the next season's bounty—the poignancy of the first taste of the year, be it fresh green peas, eggplants, chestnuts, or mandarin oranges—and of course, the accompanying aromas. Spring flower scents give way to the tang of tomato leaves in summer, then to the ubiquitous smoke of burning stubble in autumn and the purity of snowy air. Thus we reassure ourselves—because if the seasons are progressing to expectations, this old Earth, beleaguered though she may be, yet has health in her. We await the harbingers of the seasons with the confidence of children trusting in our parents' loving care.

In the countryside especially, the seasons are watched very closely. Like the plants themselves, we train ourselves to feel changes in temperature and light so that we can enjoy, at just the right moment, the plumpness of our strawberries or the sweetness of a frosted cabbage. Each season is attached to a physical memory so sharp it is like lemon pepper on the tongue. Spring is all dizzy-dazzled wandering through a riotous flower bed. Summer is sweat dripping into the eyes and the sun on our back as we work at an outdoor task. Autumn is extra coolness in the air and extra blankets on the bed. Winter is the reek of kerosene stoves and the warmth of a tea cup.

The cities do it as best they can—and they really make an effort in Japan. Department stores, supermarkets, and public places are decorated with paper and plastic seasonal tokens—the cherry blossoms, the beach ball, the chestnut, the snowflake. These, with the outdoor air temperature and the dress

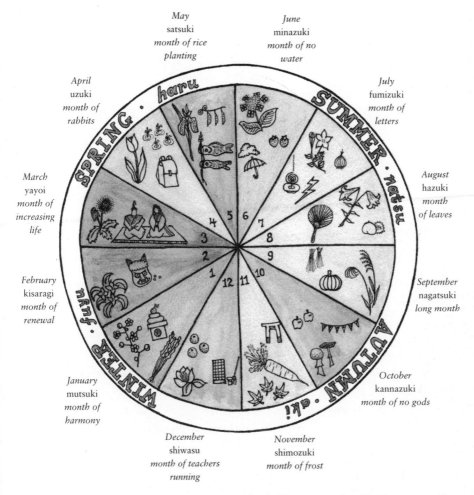

Wheel of the seasons, showing plants, vegetables and holiday decorations evoking the months

of the crowd, are the city's seasonal indicators. But if the city's seasons are a single multicolored thread, those in the countryside are an entire tapestry. It is here that I can steep myself in each season, from the colors of the mountains to the different weeds that shyly poke up between the stones. I think this richness is certainly one reason why I am glad the countryside is the scene of my Japanese sojourn. My home rewards me—pressed down, shaken together, and running over—every day, every month, and every season.

The Big Freeze

Since I came from sunny California and subtropical Queensland, it's natural that I should face the cold season in Japan with a sigh of resignation. Winter is my least favorite season, and it seems to last much, much longer than any other. It is indeed a wearisome guest, bringing along its troublesome child, snow.

We usually get three or four snowfalls a year that are deep enough to be a bother. When the snow piles up, there's a lot of work in store. Shrubs in the formal gardens must be cleared of mounded snow lest their branches break under the weight. Our old, uneven roof requires constant attention. Sliding snow may dislodge roof tiles, which fall to earth with a crash; and though we have fastened bamboo poles to the roof to keep this from happening, the poles themselves may break or fall, necessitating replacement. Laundry must be postponed due to frozen pipes, and my back aches from the never-ending chores of shoveling snow and hauling kerosene for the space heaters.

Winter can even be dangerous. We may welcome a sunny afternoon, when snow on the ground melts in little tinkling rivulets along the south-facing downhill slope from the house to the street; but those same places, early next morning, have frozen again and are treacherous with black ice. What an evil ring that phrase has—black ice! Beware! Tread softly and tread on the white, to avoid a slip and a bone-jolting fall.

Truly, this season is no fun. The interior of the house seems even gloomier than usual in contrast to the blinding white outside, and electric lights become pallid and ineffectual. During a day spent at home, there is no acting on impulse: I must plan everything half an hour in advance, starting up the heater before I can begin my activity in the appropriate room. I wear mountains of clothes, and changing them gets tiring; long underwear, lap rugs and slippers are my constant companions. I become steeped in finicky little indoor tasks, longing for the time when I will be able to kneel in the warm sun and plunge my hands into the earth once more. When will spring be here?

Yet it seems ungrateful to spend a quarter of the year in grousing. On reflection, I'm glad that at least we have snow as well as cold. I find snow, as a natural phenomenon, extraordinarily purifying and uplifting to the heart. I never lived in a snowy place as a child, and the few excursions I took with my father into the mountains were exciting, each patch of dull leftover snow along the highway a thing of mystery. The feeling that snow is magical has persisted into my present life, and when it falls, it soothes my seasonal frustration.

Snow touches every quality of this season with its wand. Winter is quiet—few birds, no bugs—but the real deep, eerie silence of winter is most piercing on a snowy morning. Even before I get out of bed, even before first light, that extra dimension of silence settles down on my soul, so that I know what I will see when I look out the window. Winter is subdued—no flowers, no brilliant leaves—but the real leaching of color comes with a snowfall. The delicate hues of winter vegetation, the tan of grass, the gray of stone, disappear into a palette of blue-white and dark sepia shadows. Winter is stripped bare—tree fingers lifted against the sky—but the true shape of foliage becomes visible when each twig and leaf holds its tiny burden of snow. The white lines lie faithfully along every branch; pine trees dress up in big shaggy clumps of white; all the angles of the palm fronds are carefully delineated. There is a precision in the sight that rivals the intricacy of summer flowers.

The broccoli and carrots in the garden are covered with deep, soft, achingly white quilts. It seems a pity to dig down and disturb them, but the snow and frost make those vegetables extra sweet and delicious. All the trashy places around a country house—the spindly remains of weeds forgotten last autumn, the wheelbarrow with a flat tire, the untrimmed hedge, old buckets, piles of sticks—are mercifully invisible. While the snow lasts, we can enjoy the illusion of a fairy-tale existence in a neat and tidy world.

In early morning, the lane outside the house is a blank slate, which is gradually etched with the record of passages throughout the day. Monstrous tire tracks, beautifully defined boot prints, the thrashing trail left by a cat,

THE BIG FREEZE 87

even tiny bird feet leave their mark. Up in the hills on my daily walk, I can discern the tracks of deer, monkeys and boars, crisscrossing the man-made road on paths of their own through the brush.

The afternoon may bring a patch of sunshine, when the snowdrifts become dazzling diamond dust, and the clear light strikes the eyes like a sword. More often, though, grey-brown lowering clouds sift down a wavering curtain of flakes, either huge and lazy or small and businesslike, obliterating my footprints and smoothing over all the various wounds made in the snow cover. Go to sleep, wait, be at peace, spring is not yet. More snow is coming.

In recent years, I've begun to see the wisdom of honoring the balances of the seasons. I've begun to ease up on myself during winter, to take my cue from slumbering Nature outside my window, and to slow down—enjoy an afternoon nap or an extra cup of tea.

Now is the time for hibernating.

Now is the Big Freeze.

Flowering

The slumber of winter is passing. Our bodies are restless, our eyes rebel against the drab hues of mud and dead grass and old snow, our fingertips tire of the tingling numbness of cold. We yearn for color, light and air.

With voluptuous, teasing slowness, with many setbacks and false starts and hitches, ever so gradually, the spring begins. March is a good word for the first month of spring, because once it gets going, it's steady, ever faster, breathtaking in its timetable of joy. From crocuses to tulips, from dull grey to soft blue, from mud brown to trembling pastels, from frigid winds to caressing warmth. The base point of the spectrum turns to gold; everything lightens and comes forward to the eye.

Through it all we wait for the star of the show—but she is still preening in the wings, taking her time, she's not ready. TV programs breathlessly predict her appearance, the local town decorations and the seasonal sweets foreshadow her shapes and colors, but the Real Thing is yet to burst upon us. Then—on a heartbreaking day of baby blue and lamb's wool white and misty vistas—we notice that those big silvery trees, which have stood motionless guarding their secret all winter, have grown a blush of purple. Before we know it, the thousands of little mauve buds have popped like popcorn and The Flowers have arrived. For the next few short days, *Sakura*, Queen Cherry Blossom, will bless us with her presence and receive our adulation.

Suddenly the most grimy, mundane streets come alive like a crowd when a celebrity appears. Between the cold concrete and the newly gentle blue spring sky, the branches hold up frothy frills of the most delicate pink, shaken and puffed by the breeze or hushed in holy stillness, creating an intricate sculpture of the very air between and among the filigrees of blossom. The sweet five-petaled, papery whitish flowers, sewn together in the center with a cross-stitch of pink, nod and shimmer on long, fragile green bunches of stems, standing out against the rough and flaky bark with its characteristic horizontal bands. So long awaited—so warmly welcomed—the cherry blossoms, often called simply *hana* (flowers), radiate the kindness of Nature, the pink-cheeked, girl-ish, giggly adorableness of all new life, and the gratefulness of warmth after winter's chill.

For Japanese people, the time of the cherry blossoms is evocative of new beginnings in all walks of life. Children in brand new school uniforms and gleaming bags walk on a carpet of fallen petals under the trees which line the grounds of every school. New-minted university students, glowing with pride, pose for photographs under soft clusters of flowers with the august walls of their chosen college in the background. Black shiny shoes and black shiny briefcases of young recruits pass beneath pink froth on the way to their first day as salaried workers. April is the doorway to both the school year and the fiscal year in Japan, and the branches of sakura always preside at the threshold.

さくら
桜

Whatever we may have to celebrate, endure, or forget, we embrace the new season with parties under the cherry blossoms. In the public parks, by day or evening, impossibly garish pink lanterns strung from tree to tree mirror the drunken glow of the faces beneath, as they sing, toast each other with sake, and feast on delicacies from layered boxes arranged picnic-style on straw mats. A passing breeze speckles the scene with whirling, fluttering petals, so much like a snow flurry that everyone gasps, and then there is a ripple of relieved laughter as we feel the blessed warmth, and remember: Winter has passed, and another year has lifted us up and bears us along on its huge, benevolent tide.

Soon the scattering of blossom becomes a steady rain. Within a few days, the whole fabulous show has pulled up stakes and withdrawn to a cooler region, moving steadily north up the Japanese archipelago in a slow wave referred to by TV announcers as the *sakura zensen* ("cherry blossom front"). The fluffy canopy of blossom is pushed aside by tender new leaves, dusky red turning to lush green, as the cherry tree steps back into its place among all the other swathes of verdure. An eyeblink of time has cradled so many events, emotions, and memories. In its wake, bemused with beauty, we shoulder our various burdens—of study, work, or planting—and walk forward into whatever the future will bring.

Close Encounters

One spring, not so long ago, some wild honeybees came and built a nest under the floorboards of the storehouse, right in the central courtyard. In fine weather they would come and go, depart and return, in and out of the two small knotholes in the old wood. Sometimes they swarmed, and their buzzing was fierce and terrible; usually it was a sleepy humming like a small motor, enlivened by the whir of individual bees—each bee's note is different— as they set off on their expeditions.

I became accustomed to their presence, sidling quietly past the nest as I hung up clothes or opened the storehouse door. They grew accustomed to me as well, zooming upward or to the side as my bulk loomed into their flight path. I didn't feel them as hazardous, though I had no idea what their activities meant. They were a small mystery living in my home. I had a strong wish to taste the honey they made, but when winter came, they got so aggressive that I was forced to get rid of them. If only they had made their nest in a less central location, they might still be peacefully working and buzzing today. I felt terrible—but I was very glad of their company during that summer, and I learned a lot from living with them.

There are many such small mysteries in this house, which, like an ancient tree with its roots deep in the earth, plays host each year to myriad lives. The creatures of the house and garden are like the plants, waiting for the proper weather and time of year to awaken and appear. I have come to mark the season with them, as my Japanese neighbors do.

The year of living creatures begins in March with the ants. On a certain sunny day they begin their nest-building among the flagstones: mostly small black sugar ants, in lines, but sometimes a huge solitary one will lumber past like a construction vehicle. Soon the newly-turned earth of the vegetable patch teems with beetles of all kinds; the ladybugs come back to the roses; white and yellow butterflies hover over the cabbages. Birdsong casts a pattern over the hitherto silent days—first the nightingale, then the cuckoo, then the skylark. The spring peepers, thumbnail-sized frogs, raise a great chorus from the rice paddy pools at night. As the season advances, spider webs mist the hedges, and the air is humming with bees, wasps, and mayflies. Lizards dart on sun-warmed wood or stone; snakes lie blissfully sunbathing on the road. In full summer, the jabbering of crows and the eerie howling of monkeys strike out against the eternal daytime background music of the cicadas—huge blundering bugs that come out of the ground, where they have slept and matured for years, fly heavily from tree to tree, and then crouch on the trunks singing their earsplitting love songs. Around the house, opening a door, I may be surprised by a frog or a praying mantis or a salamander on the lintel. Gray hopping-spiders perched on old timber walls glare at me with their tiny faces like bearded old men. Strange beautiful butterflies, staring eye patterns on their wings, get caught in the corners of sliding doors. Finally the autumn days turn crisp and clear, and with them come grasshoppers and dragonflies by day and crickets by night. From March to November, a great wave of life surges and sweeps me up and carries me along on its journey through time.

Of course, there are "bad" creatures too—annoying horseflies and mosquitoes, destructive moths, mice and moles, and startling centipedes and huge banded wasps that can deliver a serious sting. But even these I have grown used to. The woman who today can pass within a foot of a humming bees' nest with a tray full of glassware is a very different person from the little city girl who, forty years earlier, traded hair-raising children's "bug" lore and froze with terror at the first hint of a buzz. This transformation—the ability to live amid the bustle of Nature with due caution but also camaraderie—is a gift I've gladly received from my years of living here.

The Japanese "love of nature" is famous, but I think it would be more accurate to say that, in their culture, these people have always paid attention to Nature and the richness of the seasonal changes surrounding them. They seem to appreciate, at least in a poetic context, the hugeness, the benevolence, the unequivocal there-ness of life as it is lived by even the lowliest insect. Their art is full of the fine detail of nature—the curve of the iris petal, the kink of the crab's leg, the softness of monkey fur. Popular art and cartoons show little creatures such as frogs and helmet beetles in a friendly way. It is common to keep crickets and other singing insects in little wooden cages in the home. Would it be accurate to say the Japanese love the mosquitoes even as they swat them? Would they miss the "bad" creatures, if some summer, they were unexpectedly not here? Do they really "love nature" more than other cultures? There is a great deal of art to support this notion, but also, certainly, much evidence to the contrary—the treatment of farm animals and pets, which is often disturbing and sometimes scandalous, comes to mind.

Anyhow, for myself, I am grateful that life in the countryside has accustomed me to most of the manifestations of Nature. I think camaraderie is better than fear and loathing, and living here, I've been able to cross most creatures off my fear and loathing list. By the time I die, I hope this list will be a blank, and I will have learned to embrace every part of life on this planet in friendship.

The tiniest of creatures, a book mite, like a speck of dust with a destination, moves across this paper. I blow it gently away.

Bamboo

It soars, it rockets, in strong shallow curves endlessly repeated yet delicately different. It rustles, it whispers, it clacks like musical instruments from another world. It nods, it tosses, shaggy as the heads of Chinese festival lions. It streams, it billows, like storm-soaked ocean waves. Exotic as a unicorn, common as mud—it's bamboo.

One of the most venerable calligraphy panels in our house proclaims, in nearly incomprehensible script: "Look out of the gate, there is bamboo." And there is. At the southern edge of our property is a small stand of bamboo, decimated by a road-building project years ago but still graceful as ever. It reminds me every day that I live in Asia, where bamboo grows side by side with pine, both unchanging green, whether seared by sunshine or covered with snow.

Bamboo is a gorgeous plant—a fantastic, graceful giant grass, the stuff of dreams—and its role in our lives goes far beyond the aesthetic enhancement of the view. Bamboo has been called the most useful plant in the world, and this usefulness ensures that it is always a part of the rural scene in Japan. When young, the dark, fuzzy cones of the shoots—*takenoko*, "bamboo children"—can be peeled, cut and cooked in a complicated process that results in one of the favorite delicacies of spring. When it grows into a long, subtly tapered jointed stalk, it can be brought home and put to work in a variety of ways—as supporting sticks for climbing plants, and as rods to hang the laundry or reach the highest-growing persimmons or prevent snow damage to the roof tiles. Because of its lightweight flexibility, it can be made into all kinds of things—flutes, drums, wind chimes, chopsticks, tongs, spoons, cups, baskets, pot trivets, mats, furniture, incense holders, fans—the list goes on and on. Bamboo is also amazingly durable. Simple flower vases, fashioned by legendary craftsmen and aesthetes of old, have been cherished in museums and collections for hundreds of years. Traditional houses have bamboo lattices built into the walls between the beams to support the plaster. We are using bamboo laundry poles in our house that have been in place since long before I came. It is everywhere around the home, its initial fresh green mellowing to lovely ochre, then to soft grayish brown.

In country lore, a bamboo grove is said to be the safest refuge in an earthquake. The earth here is crisscrossed, under the whispering layer of dry leaves, with a maze of hardy roots that resemble flexible plastic pipe. No matter how steep the slope, the ground never slides or erodes. There is no undergrowth in a stand of bamboo, so that the eye is hypnotized by the mysterious sameness of the shifting verticals. Look up and you seem to be at the very center of a fountain, the stalks shooting skyward on every side till they explode in a firework of blinding green blades. Glance often at the leaf carpet underfoot, and put your hand to the smooth cool curve that fills your palm as satisfying as an egg, to keep from growing dizzy at the sight of joint after joint marching upward, zigzagging from pole to pole.

An especially fascinating piece of bamboo lore is that each species has its own timetable, measured in years, of setting seed; and all over the world, like a thought traversing a giant brain, the bamboo of one species will flower at the same time. In our area, every few years the normally fresh, grassy green of the bamboo forests will fade to an eerie, somber grayish ochre, which is the color of the flowering. The following year everything will be as before.

This astounding plant has many admirers. Those that have concern for our planet love bamboo, which is fast-growing, inexpensive, and prolific, and can substitute for precious trees in many applications, including paper and fabric. Botanists find it fascinating because it grows in many subtly different colors and forms, large and small, green, golden, black, striped, and spotted. Gourmets eagerly await the tender new shoots of spring, with their nutty flavor and crunchy texture, to use as an ingredient in evocative seasonal dishes. Craftsmen praise its versatility and the lovely warm color which blends so beautifully into a Japanese interior. Music lovers know that bamboo is the purest and simplest of flutes, and the haunting, softly floating timbre of the *shakuhachi* or the shrill piercing cry of the *fue* are the very essence of traditional music.

Indeed, bamboo is many things to many people. But for me, the other-worldly exotic beauty of it is the point where it enters my soul. I'm living in a place where I can look out of the gate and see bamboo.

I'm definitely not in Kansas anymore.

Autumn Leaves

Color—ah, color is what makes my artistic life worth living. I especially love mixed, variegated color—the "dappled things, things of couple-color" of the poet G. M. Hopkins—so it was a delight to discover that each season in Japan has its own distinctive palette.

The top and bottom of the ferris wheel of the seasons, predictably, are the most intensely contrasted. Riotous summer, the zenith of the year, has its swathes of flowers, tumbled together like a magician's scarves; its plump, silken vegetables shining like water balloons of purple, red and yellow; and its green, green, green. At the nadir, the winter subtleties of the different grays, duns, and browns, punctuated by calligraphy patterns of bare black branches, stark white and glinting low sunlight, are a hard-won aesthetic, a gourmet's taste. In between, on the upswing of spring, everything is new and so are the colors: yellow, pink and lavender, soft yet vivid, glowing with life from within, like a child's downy cheek. It is brief, as is the downturn of autumn, season of maturity, setting off, letting go, the sigh of parting. This last, for me, is the time when the richest spectrum may be enjoyed.

In autumn, cool breezes tantalize back into life a spirit flattened by the sun's tyranny, and curiosity and creativity can flow anew. The high, deep sky, the most pristine blue of the year, is the perfect backdrop for the earthy hues of chrysanthemums and the gorgeous pale orange globes of persimmons. As I walk along a country road, I marvel at the brocade tapestry revealed underfoot with each step—the tiny, modest autumn wildflowers, the dying grasses, the nodding seed heads. Last and best are the tonal shades of the changing trees, like the Japanese maple, which spreads its gently rustling sheaves like peacock's tails in dazzling brilliance across the sky. These leaves faithfully show the majestic passage of their master sun, with roasted scarlet on the surface, shading through vermilion and rust to pale yellow in the lower, more sheltered branches.

As a student, I used to bring a dictionary along with me on autumn walks—not to look up arcane color names, but to press the fallen leaves I gathered. The gently curving, fan-shaped golden ginkgo, the soft, tanned-leather-colored serrated chestnut, and the wildly varying colors of the maple—like snowflakes, no two were alike. Sometimes, years later, I open a dictionary and find one of these leaves, faded and brittle but still aromatic, pressed between the pages.

Yes, it's easy to wax poetic about autumn. I'm forced to disclose, however, that it does have its uncomfortable side. For one thing, in order to enjoy the wonderful changing leaves, I must first clear a space on my schedule, which is a balancing act as the slippery slide of the last brief weeks of the year escapes from under my feet, faster and busier and more breathless all the time. If I do take a few precious moments to visit a customary "famous site" for maples, I can be sure that thousands of other people will also be converging on the place. The annual autumn leaf pilgrimage mirrors the spring cherry blossom bacchanalia, but instead of the awe and adulation given to sakura, tourists on a *momiji-gari* (maple leaf hunt) unblushingly criticize the show, saying it's not as good as last year, and citing weather blips that might be responsible. Also, a recent phenomenon has tarnished the crowning glory of the year—the garish nighttime illuminations of autumn foliage in the major temples. Once a daytime sanctuary for brooding haiku poets or meditating scholars, the paths beneath these ancient trees are now mobbed by night with jostling teenage girls pressed up against their boyfriends as they gaze upward, slack-jawed, before trooping off for a bowl of noodles, or the more seasonally authentic hot, sweet red bean soup called *o-shiruko*.

Another common sight in autumn really has me wondering about the much-vaunted Japanese "love of nature". In Kyoto and other cities, the main streets are lined with ginkgo trees. Before these august and noble trees can reach the peak of their golden autumn glory (and before the fallen leaves can cause a nuisance), the branches are unceremoniously lopped off and carted away, leaving knobbly stubs in mockery of their dignity. What people could advertise their "love of nature" so assiduously and at the same time repeat such a public desecration, year upon year, in the name of convenience? I suppose "nature" means different things to different people: in Japan, it sometimes seems that nature isn't really lovable unless it can be coerced into doing the bidding of human beings.

Another facet of the Japanese attitude to nature is illustrated by a story from the world of tea. A certain tea master was well known for his garden, and especially for the gorgeous morning glories that bloomed there for a few days every year. A high official begged to be allowed to see them, and was invited to tea. On the appointed day, the illustrious guest arrived to find the entire garden stripped bare—not one was to be seen. Puzzled, he stepped into the tearoom, to be met with the sight of a single pristine bloom, occupying the place of honor in the alcove. This story is supposed to emphasize the tea master's sophisticated artistic sensibility. When I first studied tea, I thought I understood the point. Now I feel like weeping for all the flowers lying on the trash heap in obedience to an aesthetic whim. Is someone flaunting a spray of golden ginkgo leaves in his living room, as the parent tree patiently endures its grotesque nudity on the street outside?

At my house, I let my trees do as they please. They change color undisturbed by confusing lights. Their leaves fall and lie on the ground. The little wildflowers bloom and fade, and the grasses flatten and blanch. Autumn proceeds in its own way. The colors are no less glorious, the tapestry is no less vibrant, for being uncontrolled. And my conscience is clear.

Reminiscences

Photograph of my husband and me on our wedding day

Characters
for our
family name,
Otowa

Pictograms

When I entered high school in Australia, I was asked if I wanted to be in a pilot program on Japanese language. I thought about it—learning Japanese. I agreed because the idea of writing the characters appealed to me. Of course I didn't know that saying yes would determine the course of my whole life.

I was frustrated at the beginning of the course because the writing lessons proceeded so slowly. I used to corner the teacher and beg her to show me how to write things we hadn't yet learned in class. My love of Japanese writing carried me through the years of study before I came to Japan. It even survived the enormous setback of being told that brush-stroke calligraphy was all but impossible for a left-handed person. Now, in my everyday life, one of my greatest satisfactions is the ability to read—city signs, village notices, magazine articles; and, in spite of my left-handedness, to write—my address, letters to friends, talks for local groups.

Japanese writing uses Chinese characters to convey meaning, and two sets of phonetic symbols, derived from these characters, to indicate pronunciation and grammar. A literate person must therefore know over a hundred phonetic symbols and up to eight or ten thousand characters. Some Chinese characters are called pictograms because they are stylized pictures of the things they represent. This is easy to see in characters like *uma* (horse) with its four feet drumming the turf and its streaming mane and tail, or *kuruma* (wheel or cart) which looks like a bird's-eye view of a huge axle connecting two wheels and a central box. More complex ideas employ more evocative images. *Haru* (spring) is a low-angled sun viewed through thin foliage, while *tagai* (mutuality) is obviously two elements linking up with each other. Of course many concepts are too abstract for any visual reference at all; these are usually composed of many separate parts, some of which contribute to meaning and some to pronunciation. The character *isogashii* (busy) contains the elements "heart" and "die". *Owaru* (finish) is made up of "thread" and "winter".

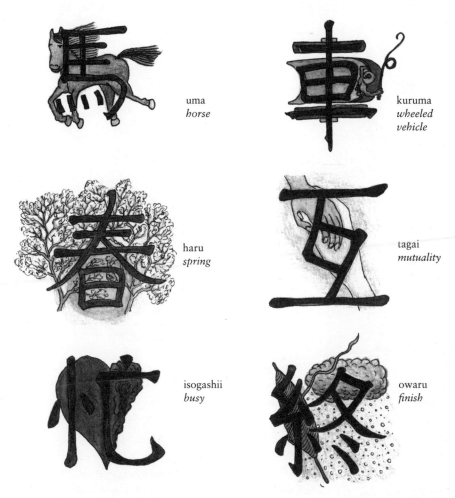

uma
horse

kuruma
wheeled vehicle

haru
spring

tagai
mutuality

isogashii
busy

owaru
finish

As we continue to learn, it becomes more and more difficult to remember which of the thousands of characters we want to use; so, like many other foreigners, I began to devise my own visual interpretations to serve as memory aids. One of the first ones I thought up was part of the word *jugyo* (lesson), which looked to me like a man sitting at a table with a standing microphone beside him. The character for *kanarazu* (without fail) seemed to be a picture of a little samurai warrior frantically waving his sword. I had no idea what the four elements of *korosu* (kill) meant, but the whole character looked so spiky and dangerous that I never forgot its meaning. Occasionally my memory aids arose out of errors. When I first saw the character *ta* (rice paddy) I thought it meant "window". After I learned the actual meaning, I thought, all right, the view from a Japanese window is likely to be rice paddies; and in fact that is the case in my life today.

ju (gyo)
lesson

kanarazu
*without
fail*

korosu
kill

ta
rice paddy

Our family name, Otowa, is made up of the characters for "sound" and "feather". The origin of this name is lost in the mists of time, since it is one of the older names in Japan (in contrast to many family names which came into use only about 150 years ago). My younger son Yuki, who practices traditional archery, considers it an eminently suitable name for an archer, whose singing arrows are tipped with owl, hawk or eagle feathers. Otowa is also the name of our village, and some distant ancestor adopted it as his own. When I write my name and address, on a bank form, or on the back of a letter, I can feel the sense of unity and belonging that this conveys, and forget, sometimes, that both the name and the feeling are borrowed for the duration.

The Wedding

In a formal garden, surrounded by shrubs of dull October green, the bride and bridegroom have been meticulously posed by the elderly cameraman. In her elaborate white costume, she is like a statue of pillows, and her face, peeping from under the silken hood, is a combination of cat-swallowed-the-canary and sheer terror. For him the soft worn silk folds of Great-Grandfather's crested wedding kimono fit much more naturally, and he is proud with the slightly scared pride of youth supported by the security of family. What a terribly revealing photograph seen at twenty-seven years' remove.

My appearance on the scene in the late 1970's as the fiancée of the best-beloved son and heir caused consternation in a family already dealing with Father's terminal illness. The union received his deathbed sanction, and having accepted the situation with reluctance, the family decided to Do Things Right. They took infinite pains to set up a highly traditional and correct wedding ceremony, with me in the center like an exotic ornament; the neighbors aflutter with helping and the shine of novelty; and the house so solid and good, like a Cave of Wonders, gold leaf gleaming and rich silk glowing in its comforting semidarkness.

The ceremony (so-called "household style", which does not involve a priest) and reception took place in what is now my living room. About fifty people were invited, with many more participating behind the scenes. It was decided that a cousin's home a few doors away was to stand in for my own (distant and nebulous as it was), and here I was dressed and prepared. Through the bright sunlight and wayward breezes, I walked in my finery with a procession of relatives, enacting the universal ritual in which a girl is passed, like a piece of fine china, from house to house before she can fall. I entered my house, as custom demanded, by the kitchen door.

As for my own family, the Japanese relatives said that their presence would be too complicated for all concerned, and so they arranged for *oya-gawari* (a substitute parent). Why did I agree to this? I can no longer remember. Most of the preparations, except for personal details of hair and costume, went ahead without me, and I did whatever I was told. Did I really feel that I was getting married? It was a huge, inscrutable Event Extraordinaire, which carried me along on its own momentum, dazed by all the tiny details which formed a hypnotic kaleidoscope of otherness.

As usual, the ordinary life that followed the wedding was a jarring descent to reality—but the sense of being swept up and carried away by my life persisted for years. It's taken me a long time to own my life here in Japan. I've had to learn how to manage the otherness of my surroundings, and how to acknowledge, even to make friends with, the persistent specter of my own ignorance.

I think one reason I was so submerged in my wedding was that I absorbed the attitude of my husband's family, whose years and tradition overpowered my featherweight American upbringing. To them, I was a foreigner whose roots and ancestors could never be known and whose parents couldn't pay their eldest daughter's wedding expenses. It must have seemed to them more like an adoption than a wedding, with the homeless and eminently malleable young waif magnanimously accepted into the centuries-old homestead. My own sense of myself sank without trace; in those early years, the few times I dared to voice my true feelings or opinions, I was scolded as though for some unpardonable rudeness.

Now, after all this time, I can begin to believe I have earned my place in the house. At any rate, in my husband's eyes, I have always been the beautiful woman and beloved wife. I didn't exchange vows with him, and most of what occurred on my wedding day was unfathomable—but still, somewhere along the line, our wedding turned into a marriage. That's because, as the central character and the root of my marriage tree, he has seen me with my own capabilities, my own bright uniqueness. He has seen me as the mother of his cherished sons. He has seen me and admired me as I deal with the everyday problems and frustrations of his home place.

He has seen me. What a relief.

Fitting In

I have always considered myself a pretty flexible person, anticipating the next new thing rather than regretting the past. I have been able to reinvent my life and to walk away from things that no longer worked for me without a backward glance. I didn't think I would have any trouble fitting in when I got to Japan. What turned out to be difficult, however, was *not* to walk away: to stick with this life I had chosen.

I look back on my childhood in the Los Angeles suburbs and see a rather solitary little girl, given to making up stories by herself. The machinations of girls' friendships were a mystery, and I found it hard to get along with them because I wouldn't follow their expectations. The few friends I recall from primary school days were boys, with whom I would shoot baskets or practice magic tricks after school. Boys were simpler. Still, I preferred solitude, in my room or my tree house, where I would read, write, and draw for hours.

I grew up feeling there was nothing particularly strange about being alone. When I first arrived in Japan, I had to start fielding the universal question, "Aren't you lonely, away from your family and friends?" and its variant, "Isn't your mother lonely with you so far away?" I couldn't figure out what they meant—this had never occurred to me. Gradually, however, these questions made me realize that I was indeed alone in a sea of Japanese.

Japan is not an easy country to be an expat in. From the day I arrived, back in 1976, I felt horribly conspicuous in crowds, my foreign proportions and coloring standing out among all those short black heads. In those days, there was none of the teenage hair-dyeing and appearance-tweaking that are so popular now; everyone seemed to be wearing a uniform. This aggressively homogeneous crowd scared me, coming from the cheery, colorful hoi polloi of subtropical Australia, where I spent my teen years. I shriveled inside when children shouted "*Gaijin*!" in the street or cowered away from me in the public bath. I became furiously modest, slinking around my neighborhood, trying to occupy as little space as possible. At the same time, my Japanese acquaintances treated me like a curiosity, and awarded me an unnatural celebrity status based on qualities I couldn't take credit for, such as my ability to speak English. I didn't realize that this treatment largely stemmed from the gaucheness of the Japanese themselves—they didn't know what to do in the face of such blatant otherness. Constantly shoehorned into this anomalous group called "gaijin" instead of being seen as myself, I really began to feel lonely.

An even more intense situation awaited me when I got married and came to live in Otowa village. Instead of being expected to be different, like an exotic zoo animal, now I was expected to be the same—in effect, to *become* Japanese—as soon as I could. My differences became flaws to be corrected if possible, barely tolerated if not. The in-laws regarded it as their mission to iron out these flaws: I was *jimi* (too subdued in my dress); I was *kawaiku nai* (unloveable); I was *okorinbo* (hot-tempered); I had a *warui kao* (bad facial expression). My fluency in standard Japanese didn't prepare me for the local dialect, and they were surprised when I didn't understand what they said. The people around me couldn't relax and neither could I, and for exactly the same reason: at any moment, I might say or do the wrong thing.

I guess the charge of okorinbo had some merit. Inevitably, I would lose my temper, especially at family get-togethers when I was expected to join in scurrying around serving the men like a proper Japanese wife. I knew men shouldn't order women around, I hated the caveman-like way they ignored me except for the most basic servitude—but I found no sympathy with the women either; they couldn't understand my objections to what seemed to them perfectly natural. It was the situation which angered me, but they all thought I was angry at *them*—Japanese people are uncomfortable with strong emotions generally, and an angry outburst is not easily forgiven.

To their credit, my female relatives wanted me to fit in because they honestly thought it would be better for all concerned. They would insist that "all" Japanese wives did this or that. Even though anyone could see, looking around the neighborhood, that this was not the case, wives who didn't behave in the perfect Japanese way were presented to me as "bad". In fact, I was becoming more Japanese as the other wives my age were steadily becoming more Western. The result is that I now have much more in common with the grannies, my mother-in-law's contemporaries. I lost the opportunity to show the women my own age what being "Western" was really like, because I didn't have enough self-confidence to take up my own heritage proudly.

Being induced to fit in with the family in this old-fashioned way was very painful and confusing. (Where was my husband in all this? Hard at work, enduring a ferociously long commute, or shuttling back and forth between my in-laws and me, trying to explain, piggy in the middle.) On good days, I imagined myself as undergoing a sort of monastic discipline, and could be grateful for *mainichi-benkyo* ("every day a learning experience"). Most of the time, however, it felt more like *mainichi-shiken* ("every day an examination")— with no graduation in sight. If I wanted to fit in, these were the terms. Somehow, I found the strength. I didn't walk away this time; I wholeheartedly committed myself to this life, warts and all.

It's taken me a long time, and a good deal of counseling, to realize what should have been obvious all along: that blind conformity isn't the best way I can contribute to my community. Maybe the judgment wasn't really that harsh, and there was never any punishment for being myself—maybe I made it all up. Who knows? These days, I've become much more fearless—more human, more vulnerable, and at the same time stronger. I realize the importance of balancing actions and reactions. Sometimes, it's better to bring out my Japanese side, to put people at their ease; other times, I enjoy throwing out a little remark to shake them up a bit.

I now see that fitting in has to include all the parts of myself, and this has to be based on my own acceptance of all those parts. I also see that the people around me are ordinary human beings, just like me, full of fears and flaws, just wanting to feel good and to belong. Come to think of it, the phrase "fitting in" has a restrictive sound; though this was the reality for me for many years, now I prefer to think of it as "embracing"—and it takes two to embrace. Me and Japan.

Motherhood

Recently I passed a daphne bush in full bloom—and I was flooded with memories. This ornamental shrub, with its clusters of tiny, pungently sweet four-petal blossoms, is one of the most beloved harbingers of spring in Japan. It is also the flower that surrounded me in the last weeks before the birth of my first son, in Kyoto, in 1983. I had lived here six years by that time, three as a student and three as a wife. After our wedding my husband and I had rented a small house on Yoshida Mountain, across the street from a quiet and picturesque old temple and close to the university where he was working on his doctorate.

My memories of being pregnant in Kyoto are mostly of walking. Kyoto is a wonderful town to walk in, and I covered many miles (between carefully spaced public lavatories) through the latter half of 1982. I walked beneath glorious scarlet maple leaves backlit by the high pure sky of autumn. I walked as I breathed the brisk, powdery, photogenic snow that falls on Kyoto. And especially, I walked as the world gradually warmed and came alive with spring. I gazed up into the branches of cherry trees and thought: By the time those buds open, I will be holding my child in my arms.

Through a friend's introduction, I was looked after by Naruse-Sensei, one of the last great midwives of Kyoto. A calm, comfortable, unfailingly polite old lady, she told me at the time that she had safely delivered over three thousand babies. Her unobtrusive little clinic had only six rooms, all with tatami floors and immaculate futons for mother and baby. It was there that the three of us—Naruse-Sensei, my husband, and I—in the deep of a spring night welcomed our son into the world. After that, I spent a luxurious week eating, resting, receiving visitors, and gazing on his sleeping face. My only problem was that I couldn't seem to finish the impossibly sumptuous meals, and that worried the midwife. Everyone around me was happy, especially my mother-in-law. She was probably remembering how joyous had been the birth of her own son, the first boy child in the house in a hundred years, the sixteenth generation of the family. Now she was seeing the seventeenth.

Myself, I do remember happiness, but that feeling was shot through with some other emotion so sharp it was like heartache. Not exactly sadness—it was the feeling of standing on a dock, watching a ship I had launched sailing away. Pride, wonder, and the agony of parting.

Taking leave of Naruse-Sensei, we carried our bundle of joy back to Otowa village. Japanese custom dictates that a woman shall spend the first weeks after birth in her mother's house; since that was not possible in my case, my mother-in-law took over. In fact, she took over much more completely than I had expected. After all, she was drawing on a wealth of experience, not only with her own children, but also nursing her own daughters after the birth of four grandchildren. I had virtually nothing to do for a month except lie in bed next to my baby, feeding and changing him. (His futons and nappies had all been hand sewn by me during my pregnancy.) Even his baths were her province—I was to watch only. Meanwhile I was barred from the family bath myself, restricted to sponge bathing for a month or so. This was only one of many reminders that in traditional Japanese culture a postpartum mother is considered unclean (which is a self-fulfilling prophecy!). I was also forbidden to read, as this was believed to weaken the eyes and sap the strength. I spent many long hours listening to the spring storms buffeting the house, mostly alone with my sleeping child. I realize now that my mother-in-law must have been frantically busy preparing for the rice planting.

It was a relief to get back to my own little house in Kyoto and take my son out to enjoy the blissful days of May. Thus began the life that has shared mine for twenty-seven years. I feel as if my son's experiences as a child in Japan were also mine, since all of its elements—playmates, games, school, sports, examinations—were as new to me as they were to him. We had problems, moments of sadness and frustration, but also successes, moments of pride and euphoria. Through it all, I was made to feel in my bones the truth of the proverb, "He who teaches children learns more than they". Seeing Japan through his eyes, I saw so many more facets of that particular diamond than I had ever known existed. At the same time, he saw Japan through my eyes, and got a broader perspective on what it means to be a human being, in this culture or anywhere.

And now, as the time of the daphne comes around once again, our journey together is over. He has come up through Japanese public school, graduated from university, and joined the international division of a company; this year he takes a wife of his own. His life has been rich so far. He has studied piano, sung in a choir, been on the high-school baseball team, written award-winning speeches in English, traveled to many countries, learned to cook, dance, and drive, acted on stage, played soccer, snowboarded, fallen in love. The ship I launched is now sailing off under his own power, full of hope and determination. So much like his dad—so much like me—so much like himself. I could wish for nothing sweeter than for his own children to give him the joy he has given me.

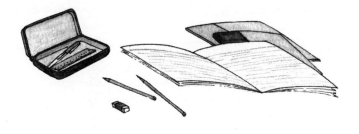

Book Learning

There is a small primary school about a kilometer down the road from our house. It is a peaceful, wide-open place, an L-shaped white two-storey building flanked by an earth playing field, swimming pool, and kindergarten complex. Cherry trees are lined up on the perimeter, poised to signal with their blossoms the beginning of each new school year. Many family connections bind us to this school: my father-in-law taught here and eventually became the principal, and my mother-in-law, her siblings, and her children all attended.

When my elder son reached school age, we decided to live in the village rather than in the city close to my husband's job. Every decision closes some doors and opens others. In our case, this decision closed the door on the possibility of "international" school, an amenity found only in far-off cities at that time. The trade-off was the overall atmosphere of country life. The kids would be among well-known neighbors and relatives, safe in a low-crime environment, surrounded by clean air, good water and food, with magnificent mountain views from every classroom window. Also, by living here full-time, they could come to understand the centuries-old continuity of our house and family. In this choice, the village won hands down.

I had no notion what to expect when I brought my five-year-old to kindergarten on an April day in 1987. As I listened to the parents' orientation, I marveled at how much was expected of children and parents alike. There seemed to be an inordinate amount of clothes-changing, and especially shoe-changing, throughout the school day. There were "inside" shoes, toilet slippers, and later, shoes for the gymnasium. All these shoes of course had to be replaced as children grew. (Were the schools in league with the shoe manu-facturers?) There were so many objects to keep track of: bags, hats, tooth-brushes, hand towels, seat cushions, special pencils and notebooks and art equipment, musical instruments, even floor-wiping rags for when the children took turns cleaning the school during the after-lunch break.

The parents (read: mothers) had their obligations too. Irritatingly, the school days always seemed to end at different times, so that mothers (or babysitting grandmothers) were stuck at home in the afternoons awaiting the children's return. There were PTA committee offices, with massive time commitments, to be undertaken by parents in turn, as well as cleanup days, school trip chaperonage, summer swimming pool detail, summer homework supervision, summer group exercise attendance… a tidal wave of responsibil-ity. The summer vacation, already only six weeks long, shrank to nothing. It was a struggle, albeit a worthwhile one, to take my kids on extended sum-mer holidays abroad every few years, so they could get some time with their "other" family, and incidentally, some perspective.

As the children learned, sometimes with great difficulty, to take control over their physical environment, they also found themselves with equally dif-ficult social requirements. The English word "education" literally means "to lead out of ignorance", but the Japanese equivalent *kyoiku* means "teach-ing and bringing up", with more emphasis on socialization. It wasn't that the teachers were strict, or punishment harsh—it was more that the children were being taught, by both overt and covert means, to be compliant, useful members of the Group. Society in Japan is supposed to be the source of all good things—as long as the members obey the rules and never question the Group's authority. I was intrigued, and impressed, by some aspects of this at my sons' school: the emphasis on taking turns, the care for younger pupils, the assumption of many responsibilities by students. However, it seemed that the children were being taught these skills not so much for the development of their individual character, as for the benefit of the Group (both in school and later in life). What I thought of as essential abilities—to make moral choices, develop a questioning mind, exercise individual integrity, and enjoy self-realization—got much less attention in Japanese school.

This sounds harsh—and many times, it was. In order to mold children to the Group, uniformity was encouraged, which showed its dark side in in-tolerance of differences. With me as their mother, my kids had their share of being chased home by older kids yelling "Gaijin!" I knew I had to do some-thing to counteract this. Finally, at my mother-in-law's suggestion, I started a primary-level English conversation class in my home and made the neighbor children welcome, so that they could see for themselves just what kind of being this gaijin was. It was a precious opportunity: after all, I was the only non-Japanese person for miles around. There's a whole generation of kids in this area whose experience of foreigners began with "Rebecca-sensei", linking my name to the word for teacher.

These days, I teach university students, and have a chance to see how the methods of Japanese early education turn out. Generally, the students are well-behaved, in a passive way, with little mental curiosity or imagination, and extremely sensitive to judgment, like head-shy puppies. Many of them seem to use their intellect in cynically second-guessing the requirements of the teachers, rather than in positively setting out to learn. I have also noticed, in adult groups I have joined, that "the way it's always been done" crushes the life out of most suggested innovations. Ironically, mindless adherence to the Group eventually ends up hurting the group, by stultifying its self-reflection and thus its progress.

I think of Japanese education as "book-learning" because it tends to operate "by the book", discouraging individuality and rewarding unquestioning obedience. Any attempt at change is largely cosmetic, with few long-lasting effects. For example, there were attempts to adopt "American-style" education, with its supposedly more relaxed atmosphere and emphasis on individuality; but the only real change we saw was the cessation of Saturday classes and this was hotly contested by teachers and parents. (At the same time, in an almost laughable reversal, American educators noticed the high test scores in Japan and showed signs of adopting a more rigid style.)

I didn't have the chance to send my boys to schools in other places, so I have only my own experience to go on. Japanese school did teach me something, however, and that is the importance, for a child, of the tempering influence of home life. I encouraged my kids to use their brains to think about the rigid school requirements, and to use their hearts to find the humanity beyond the Group. I also tried to show them how to grow up comfortable with their unique characters and contributions. Education doesn't just happen at school, and responsibility for it must be shared. The universal goal of vital, loving, courageous, considerate, creative human beings comes from the dedication, on the part of all the adults around him, to the spirit of the child.

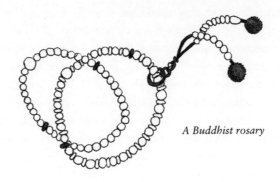

A Buddhist rosary

A Death in the Family

In a Japanese country village, death involves everyone in a widening circle of connection and obligation. When someone dies, every fellow villager is informed within hours through the telephone network, and knows the times of the wake and funeral. A monetary donation to offset costs is put into a ritual envelope and delivered to the deceased person's home on the morning of the funeral. Attendance at the funeral itself depends on relationship to the deceased, but usually most people who are at home that day are on the scene, either as mourners or as behind-the-scenes helpers. Families in the same neighborhood block as the deceased have special tasks, including preparing meals for the relatives and small gift bags for the mourners, and assisting with the monumental job of keeping track of money.

If we are connected only by village ties, the obligations end that day. If the death has been in our own family, however, a funeral is a major disruption in life, lasting up to several years. In the countryside, funeral services are usually held in the home, with several dozen guests who must be offered a meal and presented with the customary take-home gifts. When that eons-long day is finally over, there are still numerous memorial services, at increasing intervals (the final one is around fifty years after the death) also to be held in the home, with varying numbers of guests. This social disruption must be endured on top of the natural emotional disruption of grief, guilt, or unfinished business when we say goodbye to a loved one. It is a heavy burden, but one the

Japanese seem to shoulder willingly—a funeral is the social event, above all others, that everyone will drop everything to attend.

I had never been to a funeral at all before I came to Japan. The first few I attended here seemed like huge icebergs of custom and tradition with only the merest fraction visible to me. At these funerals of distant relatives, I attended either as a guest, or as the youngest and most clueless member of the kitchen staff, thrust into corners and given tasks that even I couldn't foul up, watching the busy comings and goings of the more capable wives in utter incomprehension. I couldn't learn from my experiences because I had no context to fit them into.

Thus I was unprepared for the day my mother-in-law passed away after a prolonged illness. I was already frazzled from lack of sleep and the strain of having a dying person in the house, to say noth-ing of the frayed emotions of those around me.

My own house became strange to me as it was relentlessly com-mandeered by funeral directors and neighbors, who bustled around draping walls with white sheeting, laying down dark blue carpet, unceremoni-ously shoving furniture out of the way or commenting on my sketchy housekeeping in clearly audible tones. I was the wife of the house, but I was helpless. Everyone approached me with questions—where were certain objects kept? Did I have any other tea besides this? I began to sound just as stupid as I felt, my Japanese deserting me through sheer exhaustion. My sisters-in-law tried to explain, but their words fell on my ears like the soothing of crazy-house doctors. It was the worst time in my life in Japan so far. I have never felt so unnecessary

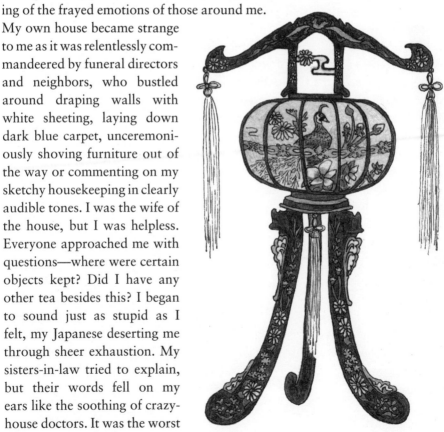

Lantern used at household altar at a funeral ceremony

and useless. None of the skills I had honed over forty-three years of life could get me through this situation. And I was distracted from the important task of sorting out how I felt about my mother-in-law who was gone.

Now, several years and numerous memorial services later, my store of funeral-related knowledge has grown. I know, to a certain extent, which utensils, dishes, cushions, screens and altar equipment to prepare; which envelopes should be used for which money; where and when and how to exchange the ritual greetings. I can even distinguish among the chanted Buddhist texts, and I know which one signals a break in the obsequies and the offering of tea and sweets. Of course I am aware that, far from becoming one of the superwomen who carry the whole event safely to a respectable conclusion, I will always be on the margin of activity—but it's more comfortable there. Anyway, I will never again have to live through that Kafkaesque nightmare of being simultaneously on the inside and the outside. For better or for worse, I'm on the inside now.

These days, a lot of these customs are changing, and even such minimal knowledge as I possess, hard-won though it is, will certainly be obsolete in a few years. Already the first public funeral home has opened in our town, requiring major adjustments to ceremonial logistics and accepted social forms. By the time my children are preparing to bid their final farewells to me, a good deal less ritual and rigmarole will be involved. As with many other vanishing social customs, what we gain in simplicity and convenience we will lose in family and village interrelationships. However, the decrease in social obligations may free us to concentrate on the essentials in the momentous task of ushering a fellow human being out of this world.

Lessons
from Japan

*Japanese traditional
card game, hanafuda
(flower cards)*

The Japanese Heart

As a foreigner who speaks Japanese fluently, I have often had the chance to give talks to local groups. Recently I was asked to address the International Association of a neighboring town, and was given a theme—"Take Back the Japanese Heart". Initially I felt it was rather presumptuous to be lecturing people on the state of their hearts; but gradually I became fascinated by the idea of analyzing the sustaining emotional energies of the people I live with.

The heart is a very private arena, and one we hesitate to reveal to anyone outside our circle of intimates. This is especially true of the Japanese. Over the centuries of their tumultuous history, they have evolved an effective defense system to protect their central constellation of emotions. In fact, these defenses work so well that in the global human family, the Japanese have a reputation for being rigidly self-controlled, unemotional, or even cruel. My life among them has shown me a completely different side. Of course, since they are human, some feelings that begin as pure or positive are warped out of shape by insecurity, fear, or desire—but the basic components of their hearts, as I have experienced them, are as follows.

At the core of the Japanese heart is a search for *wa* (peace or harmony), which manifests itself in all areas of life. There is a strong urge for harmony with a benevolent Nature, and this takes the form of gratitude to the gods that are supposed to infuse natural phenomena—gratitude for life, in fact—and the resulting outpouring of exquisite art. This evokes the desire for harmony with others, to share one's life and participate consciously in society. In order to achieve harmony with one's group, effort is necessary: to pull one's own weight, suppress individual desires, minimize disruptions, and contribute to the smooth flow of group energy. This very effort produces a need for a more private harmony, with the self and with one's intimates, which softens and makes bearable the demands of a hierarchical, group-oriented society. One can sympathize with others' tribulations, and receive sympathy in return. This appears as the national trait of *amae* (dependence), an attempt by the sensitive heart to return to the warmth and security of childhood and mother's love. These warm feelings lead into harmony with physical existence: the deep appreciation of bodily comfort and pleasure, as seen in the refreshingly guilt-free enjoyment of food, alcohol, beauty, fellowship, sex, the bath, and relaxation. In a state of pleasure, the heart returns to the feeling of gratitude for life and for one's surroundings. In this way the various emotions rotate around the central core, which is the search for harmony, providing the emotional energy of the Japanese psyche.

Harmony with the Body

気楽
kiraku
comfort

Harmony with the Gods

感謝
kansha
gratitude

和
wa
harmony

同情
dojo
sympathy

努力
doryoku
effort

Harmony with the Individual

Harmony with the Group

Diagram of the Japanese heart , kokoro, as I conceived it for the talk

Maybe this sounds presumptuous, after all—and simplistic as well. But every individual experience of reality produces an individual ordering of reality. Over my thirty years of life here, I have been thrown together with the people around me in many different situations, and I often wondered what made them tick. Preparing for this talk enabled me to organize my impressions into a coherent form, which happily turned out to be beautiful and satisfying as well as useful. The talk was quite a success. I realized that far from being offended, the audience appreciated a fresh and original view of something they may never have consciously considered.

I think I understand my family and neighbors better now.

Porcelain tea service for guests

Everyday blue-and-white ware

Tea

Imagine a well-appointed, doily-draped reception room within a large and distinguished company. Seated on a black leather sofa, the visitor looks up as the door opens to admit a uniformed young woman carrying a small round tray. With unobtrusive politeness she bends, places a small handleless ceramic cup resting on a wooden saucer before the guest, then straightens, bows, and withdraws. The guest lifts the hot cup between his fingertips and feels his spirit go quiet as he sips the light green, gently steaming brew.

Now imagine another scene: a tiny, rustic hut, placed with exquisite care amid the nodding fronds and velvet mosses of a formal garden. Behind the closed door, in the diffuse light of paper screens, the guest sits, upright but relaxed, in exactly the right spot on the tatami. With stylized yet natural motions, he picks up the rough pottery bowl presented by the host sitting opposite, and raises it to his lips, partaking in precisely three and a half sips of the few tablespoons of warm, frothy, astringent green liquid in the bottom.

Both of these scenes are immediately familiar to any Japanese. The ritual of *omotenashi* (hospitality) is at the core of each, with green tea as the elixir that symbolizes the acceptance of guest by host. In this atmosphere—warm and cool, intimate and remote, simple and deep—the best minds can meet and communicate. Compared to other drinks of hospitality, coffee and alcohol, which have an exciting and even manipulative effect, tea seems to be of the spirit. At the same time, it is also deeply familiar and loved by everyone, from the grade-school child to the grandmother, from the construction worker to the diplomat. It is the beverage of Japan.

Tea plantations, the low, contiguous small-leaved bushes hugging the hill-sides like wide-wale corduroy, are a feature of the landscape in many areas. As well, private homes in the countryside may have at least a few tea bushes on the property, and my own is no exception. For years, early in my marriage, I helped with the tea harvest in May, when the soft, tender young leaves unfurled from the darker green of the old growth below. Hoisting the round bamboo basket over my shoulder in the glorious spring sunshine, or sitting in the shady entryway ploughing my hands through the huge pile of cool, damp cut leaves to remove sticks and snails, I gratefully absorbed the essence of spring with every breath of the silky scent. At the end of the day's work, we would stuff the leaves into cloth bags, and take them to the processing barn in the next town. Several days later, we would receive a much smaller paper bag of dried tea leaves (which had been steamed, instead of being roasted as black tea is), to be stored in a foot-high square metal can—our tea for the year.

Tea harvesting time made me recall the years I spent at a traditional "tea ceremony" school in Kyoto, when I was a student. At first, I was preoccupied with learning to use the special bamboo whisk to whip the mixture of powdered tea and hot water into a lovely moss-like green froth (while trying to ignore the protests of my folded legs as I maintained the formal sitting posture). Soon, however, I realized that the study of tea was much more than this. It was here that I first experienced the uniquely Japanese meditation based on the "form" of movements, and was awakened to the uniquely Japanese aesthetic appreciation of *wabi-sabi* (the poor, the irregular, and the plain). It was a chance to become familiar with many artistic fields—ceramics, textiles, painting, calligraphy, flower arranging, incense, and sweets, which all have their tea-related forms and fashions. As well, it was a history lesson. I learned that green tea was brought to Japan from China in the early twelfth century and first cultivated at a temple near Kyoto. (One of my most precious student memories is of staying at that temple and helping to serve tea to guests enjoying the autumn foliage.) With its fundamentally Zen Buddhist philosophy, the Way of Tea gradually evolved into a complex rite of hospitality, adopted by political and military leaders, and at its height in the sixteenth century was a system of great power. Knowledge of tea is still considered an important sign of a proper upbringing; it certainly made a good impression on my boyfriend's mother when we first met.

Although we seldom harvest tea at our house these days, the bushes remain—gnarled, knee-high, many-branched, persistently putting forth the glossy, cushiony, serrated leaves and the small, waxy white flowers (reminiscent of its cousin, the camellia) and the grayish, nutmeg-like seed pods. The tea bushes are a reminder to me of the sacred covenant between host and guest in bygone days, and the importance of omotenashi, which continues to elevate human meetings into the realm of ritual.

Silk pouch for tea container

Bamboo tea whisk

17th century Korean tea bowl, Kizaemon

Utensils used in the tea ceremony—tea caddy, tea whisk, and bowl

Ceremonial wooden box used for drinking sake

Artisans

In our town, the main shopping thoroughfare is festooned with hundreds of sprays of plastic foliage, fastened to the street lighting poles and changed each season by the local Merchants' Association. These decorations are part of the regular background of town life, mostly unnoticed, providing a continuous punctuation of color along the street. In autumn, they are hot red, orange and yellow; in winter sparkling silver and white; then the candy-pink flowers of spring give way to the rich multihued green of summer. They are a stylized representation of the changes of season taking place in real life just beyond the rows of buildings. Some may think them tacky or vulgar, but they represent a strong and ever-present impulse to beautify the everyday surroundings.

Artistry is everywhere in Japan. It is in the delicately patterned and meticulously folded gift wrappings in the department stores, and in the subdued mottled brown of dried bamboo leaves enclosing steamed rice cakes. It is in the lavish gold-thread-embroidered stage curtains in the auditorium, and in the humble dark blue noodle shop curtains splashed with white calligraphy. It is in the subtly blended glaze of the valuable ceremonial tea bowl, and in the homey blue-and-white porcelain of the breakfast tea cup. No matter how mundane their function may be, many household items effortlessly display that essentially Japanese touch of evocative, stylized beauty in color, shape, and design.

The pursuit of beauty in this culture is a sturdy tree that over the centuries has absorbed influences from many rich sources and blossomed into many diverse aesthetic elements. The element of *miyabi* (gorgeousness) shines out in the priceless kimono fabric, with its exquisitely contrasting swirls of color picked out with gold and silver thread, or the quirky, sharply angled scenes of court interiors painted on the deep gold leaf background of the folding screen. At the other end of the beauty spectrum, the heavy, earthy red and black irregularity of Bizen pottery and the rustic straw basket vase, the thatched roof of the hut with the globes of orange persimmons hanging like lanterns against a high autumn sky, are examples of the element of *wabi-sabi*, or rustic simplicity. The ache in the heart evoked by the cry of wild geese across the full moon, the white crane standing stock-still in the daybreak river, or the serried ranks of bamboo-covered mountainsides receding one by one into the mist—this is the element of *yugen* (remoteness). And the poignancy of impermanence, the sweet vulnerability of imperfection, so different from the idealistic ultimatums of Western traditional aesthetics, these feelings have a name as well—*mono no aware*, the sadness of "all things must pass". Japanese people may not all know the technical terms for the enjoyment of their cultural aesthetic, but they all seem to feel that a little artistic refinement is a natural and pleasurable part of life, and they incorporate it wherever they can.

Kokeshi *doll*

Many people don't stop at mere observation, but get actively involved in artistic pursuits. In autumn, the burst of energy that accompanies blessedly cooler weather is universally acknowledged and channeled into two great streams of human endeavor— athletics and art. The athletes may have garnered cheers and prizes when they crossed the finish line in October, but the "Culture Day" exhibitions held in November at every town hall, high school and university are a chance for the non-athletes to display their accomplishments in a wide variety of art forms. Members of countless "circles", each devoted to a different medium—painting of all kinds, calligraphy, photography, paper and fabric crafts, weaving, pottery, woodwork, glassware, and many others, both indigenous and foreign—prepare their year's projects. The performing arts are also repre-sented at Culture Festivals, with groups breathlessly waiting at the edge of the stage to perform their vocal or instrumental music, their traditional or mod-ern dance, their comedy skits or *rakugo* monologues, their drums or flutes or *koto* harps. The artisans and the performers are ordinary people. They may be overworked company stalwarts or stay-at-home moms, high school students or retired grandfathers, but they all take that evening or weekend chance to escape from their everyday lives into the world of art.

This is one aspect of my life that has been utterly changed by living here—my eye for beauty. When I return to my home country, I can't be transported by everyday objects, which seem to me either uninspired or garishly over-decorated. My soul is steeped in Japanese beauty. It is colored delicate moss green and rich plum purple, vibrant black and stunning vermilion. I am one in spirit with the Europeans of two centuries ago, hopelessly, joyfully addicted to the "Japonesque".

Footwear used with kimono—tabi socks and zori shoes

The Three D's of the Kimono

It's graduation day at the university. The air is balmy for March. Steady streams of people move against the sunlit grey walls toward the broad steps of the hall, pride and happiness rising from them like incense. Among the loud-laughing, dark-suited boys and the quietly glowing parents dressed in their sober best, the figures of the kimono-clad girls illuminate the crowd in vivid splashes of color. Their kimono fluff and fledge in the breeze, sleeves and hem pliant as water. They step delicately on small white-toed feet, swaying like young trees, the body line a straight bole firmly held at the waist with the stiff ornate sash a hand-span wide, tied into a huge sculpture of a bow at the back.

Look at this one. For this day, she has been transformed. Instead of her everyday black and grey, she is dressed in magenta, primrose, turquoise and plum. Her usual akimbo stance, the careless walk with pointy shoes flapping, the gum-chewing face hovering transfixed over her mobile phone—all have been covered in gorgeous layers of silk-like frosting. But she is a modern girl, and sometimes the cake shows through. She is used to moving freely, and kimono is a Discipline. Like most high-class women's apparel of any age and culture, kimono, to make the proper visual statement, requires a certain form and carriage of the body, a certain length of step and angle of foot. It's hard for this girl to assume a behavior that matches the kimono—a couple of evenings' fond tutelage by her mother cannot substitute for the unconscious grace of lifelong habit that this costume both required and produced in days gone by.

In spite of her occasional awkwardness, however, her face shows that she is dreaming of a bygone age, when the privilege of decking oneself in a beautiful and expensive ensemble did in fact make a statement (and not just a financial one) about the girl wearing it. She could be a fairy-tale princess or a sheltered, pampered daughter of a great house, instead of another middle-class girl who has struggled for job placement like the rest and in a week must join the workforce. Right now, she feels pretty and her dreams can fly—for kimono is also a Disguise, which can dissolve the wearer's identity in a warm bath of imagination.

After a few hours of exaltation, the ceremony and family photographs concluded, she is glad, oh, so glad, to be free of her silken finery, which has begun to constrict her breathing and is distracting her with the awareness of the hot, wrinkled layers around her waist. To leave the grace and majesty in a many-colored puddle on the floor, to resume the blessed ease of the black and gray, the gum and the mobile phone, and go off to a party with her friends, is an inexpressible relief. The truth is that there is Discomfort in squeezing oneself into an unaccustomed form for too long. The photographs remain, and are treasured—but they are like hermetically sealed crystals of beauty. The rarified atmosphere of kimono belongs to the world of special occasions, and it has no place in the breathless onward rush of her real life.

I wore kimono almost every day when I studied at a tea ceremony school in Kyoto. We foreign pupils were expected to wear the outfit to class, and to care for its many components, as part of the broad spectrum of tea-related study. Our upper-classmen would help and tutor us in the complex procedure of putting it on, from the gauze undergarments with their waist-constricting ties, to the precise angle of the stiff white collar which stood up, slightly off the nape, like a silken wall. The sash, several meters long, wound us around and around, layering the waist till it disappeared and the simple straight line, from throat to ankle, was produced. The tightly tucked skirt portion, together with the uncomfortable footwear (traditionally a size too small), ensured that we would have to adopt the short, mincing, pigeon-toed walk that showed off the ensemble to greatest advantage. The dressing process, with more than a dozen separate pieces, usually took us about half an hour. Undressing after class was much easier, but once all the layers and ties had been blessedly removed, we had the chore of folding the garments back into their special folds and replacing them in their rice-paper packages till next time (kimono are always folded for storage, rather than hung on hangers).

My experience of the three D's of kimono is now in the past—the last time I wore one was at my mother-in-law's funeral ten years ago. I graduated from the Discipline, thankfully said goodbye to the Discomfort, and, finally, put the possibility of Disguise behind me as well. Although I love the sight of a well-dressed Japanese lady, and I'm grateful for the experience, I can't cover over my own foreignness with layers of silk—kimono really does require a certain body type and proportion. I'll never be Japanese, and now I can see that truth clearly and without regret. I've decided not to wear kimono any more—it's a kind of symbol of my self-acceptance.

Sweets

The Japanese word for "sweet" is *amai*. The word also has the connotation of "making things easy"—and in many ways, this is the place of sweets in Japanese culture. They are offered in circumstances that must be marked by a ritual exchange, such as meetings, returning home from a trip, weddings, and even funerals. There are special sweets whose color and shape instantly remind us of some slice of life—the *tsuru-kame* (crane and turtle) motif of weddings; the congratulatory plants *sho-chiku-bai* (pine, bamboo, and plum) of New Year; lotus plants, invoking the Buddha, for the O-Bon festival when the dead visit the living. Sweets are also fashioned into an endless variety of other forms from nature, calling forth the feelings of the different seasons. Pink and yellow flowers of spring, watery blue ripples of summer, crimson maple leaves of autumn, dark earth dusted with snow in winter—all are evoked by sweets at the proper time. And year-round, each region turns a brisk trade in local *meibutsu-gashi* (specialty sweets), sold to visitors as a memento of their stay, and often stamped with an image of a castle, scenic view, or historical figure of the area.

All this variety bewilders the eye and lures the palate into anticipating that these sweets, which are so vastly different visually, will also have very different flavors. In reality, however, the taste of Japanese sweets is remarkably homogeneous, reminding me that the triumph of form over substance is a recurring theme of life here. No one would deny that food should be a feast for the eye; in this case, it is definitely the eye that has the advantage, at least in the experience of my own Western-tutored palate. For a truly enjoyable sweet-eating experience, the extra ingredient of ritual significance seems to be needed. These are not snacks to be munched while watching TV. The flavor is enhanced by the formal sitting posture, the company, the polite phrases, the gently steaming tea in the best cups, and the view of the garden.

The list of materials for traditional Japanese sweets is very short. Sugared pastes made from *anko* (red or white beans), about the consistency of a soft cheese, predominate, along with o-mochi, which is soft, sticky and doughy. There are also gelatins and various flours made from rice, wheat, and beans. Other flavors such as *miso,* cinnamon, salted preserved leaves, or chestnuts, in small amounts, provide some variety. The main standbys of Western candy-making—fruit, dairy products, and cocoa—are usually not to be found. Japanese confectionery seems intensely sweet to me, but these people insist that Western cakes and candies taste sweeter because they contain animal fats, which their Japanese counterparts never do. The heaviness of the *omogashi* ("main" sweets) described above is balanced by the delicate *higashi* ("dry" sweets), which are small, crunchy or crumbly, and often resemble Western-style cookies or spun sugar, in exquisite shapes. Both types are used in the tea ceremony to prepare the palate before the whipped tea, which would otherwise be too bitter, is enjoyed.

Where do these sweets come from? The pink and white congratulatory sweets in their red lacquer boxes obviously have their origin in China, whereas there is a definite native sensibility in sweets shaped like pine needles or autumn leaves. Interestingly, some of the best-loved sweets are actually European in origin, such as *Castella* (rendered in Japanese as *kasutera*), a square-cut pound cake, or *confait* (*konpeito*), tiny hard colored spiky balls of crystallized sugar, which both were introduced from Portugal hundreds of years ago. These days, too, there is a tendency to incorporate Western ingredients—the well-loved, pillowy *daifuku mochi* may now contain strawberries or even pineapple, and there are versions of higashi with chocolate flavoring.

Painstakingly shaped, delicately colored, beautifully presented, and ritually consumed, sweets are Japanese artistry in edible form. I love to look at them, but when a visitor brings a large flat box in gorgeous wrapping paper to my house, I must confess I hope for cookies rather than these sweets. Perhaps the tongue lags behind the eye in assimilating a different culture. Still, I do appreciate people who can incorporate an earthy physical pleasure like the consumption of sweets into their rituals.

 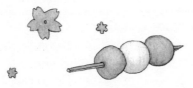

Spring sweets— sakura-mochi *and* hanami-dango

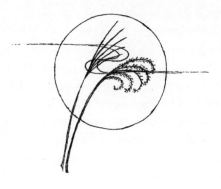

Moon Viewing

One evening, as we were enjoying the crisp autumn air, I finally succeeded in showing my son the Man in the Moon. "See," I said, "he's turned slightly to the left and his eyes are deep-set and shadowed." He smiled slowly in comprehension. "I can see his nose," he said.

At that time the Moon and Mars were in such close conjunction that the full Moon's pallid disc actually obscured Mars for an hour or so. Earlier, as I drove home from work, I saw the pair of them in the sky over the eastern mountains, wreathed in soft clouds. I smiled at the tableau they made, the Man in the Moon seeming to glance down at little Mars which rolled like a pebble at his feet. Later, standing in an ocean of cricket song and silvery light, washed by waves of autumn's grateful coolness, I gazed up at that inscrutable face that has seen everything that has ever happened on Earth.

This is the season when the Moon is at its most beautiful—when, in days of old, *O-tsuki-mi* (Moon-viewing) parties were held, poetry composed, special sweets enjoyed, and sake drunk. The soft, yielding pampas grass that grows in autumn looks perfect nodding across the full moon's surface, and there is a magical quality in the night air at this season that brings poetry bubbling to the surface of the soul.

When the Japanese look up at the Moon, what they see is not a jovial, benevolent Man. Their culture trains them to see a scene of a rabbit pounding o-mochi in a huge wooden mortar. This scene is canted over to the right, so the rabbit and his mortar seem to be stuck up on a wall, which makes the scene hard for Westerners to discern; but Japanese people, including my son, have told me they find the eminently visible Man in the Moon equally difficult to see. Thus in Japanese culture, rabbits and the Moon are a paired image, and rabbits have borrowed from the Moon that air of drowsy and remote mystery, that dreamlike quality, that wash of illusion.

The full Moon also speaks to the Japanese heart in the language of the circle, symbol of plenitude and completeness. *Maru* (the circle) is how the Zen masters pictured the universe. Maru is how the Japanese schoolteachers mark the right answer, and it is included in the names of ships to ensure the vessel will make a circle, going out and then coming back. Maru is good and right and infinitely desirable, the symbol of everything that makes life worth living.

An old children's song sums up that dreamy, contented, peaceful, just-going-to-sleep feeling. Autumn is here and the coolness of the night breeze is perfect for sleep. And when we sleep, we dream of silent rabbits bounding endlessly through celestial fields.

Children's song for the moon

The Moon has come out,	*Deta deta tsuki ga*
Round, round, perfectly round,	*Marui marui man-marui*
The Moon is like a tray.	*Bon no yo na tsuki ga*
The Moon is hidden	*Kakureta tsuki ga*
Black, black, perfectly black,	*Kuroi kuroi makkuroi*
The clouds are like ink.	*Sumi no yo na kumo ni*

Changes

A winter scene of our house

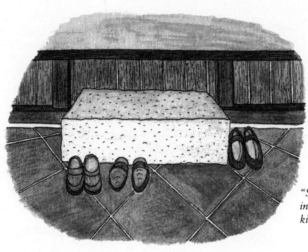

The Body

It's morning, and I'm sitting in the small glass room that I call my "office". I have to close the blue curtains at this hour in order to shade my page from the sun's glare. My black-and-white cat has just come in to nap on my big chair. The spiky shadow of the bouquet of pencils and brushes in the oversized coffee cup falls across the long-suffering wood surface of my work table. Outside the window, my weedy back garden, with its rows of low tea bushes, *yuzu* and laurel, plum and azalea, cherry and scented olive, enjoys the soft spring air. It's the kind of scene you might see in any writer's room anywhere in the world. So what would set me apart (aside from the Japanese vegetation)? How does it feel, moment to moment, to be me? How am I different from what I would have been had I never come here, never elected to spend my life in this foreign land?

We all regenerate every cell in our bodies every seven years, I've heard; if so, I've grown a new body four times over since I've been in Japan, and each time my cells have become more permeated with the air, water, and rhythms of this part of the world, like a sponge gradually soaked in wine. My body has been shaped by its environment in many different ways. Here are a few of them.

- As I sit with my legs folded under me on the faintly resilient (but not resilient enough!), slightly ridged surface of a tatami mat, my ankles and knees send out whispers of protest which escalate through levels of distracting discomfort to the demand to move NOW—RIGHT NOW. After years of life on the floor, my ankle bones have big pads of callus on them, and my knees emit a surreptitious melody of mysterious twinges and creaks whenever I move.

- My feet are exquisitely attuned to the difference between outdoors and indoors. They know that if no shoes are placed at one of the dozen or so doorways in the house, I can't go outside at that point. The shoes live "below", and are forever banished from "above", the living area raised about half a meter from the ground. Wearing clompy, heavy, DIRTY shoes in the house now feels to me as peculiar as going barefoot outside.

- Almost every light switch in the house is in the form of a cord hanging down from the fixture itself—in the middle of the room. My body has had to learn the precise location of every piece of furniture so as to avoid crashing into it in the dark, as I advance with hand outstretched, swiping back and forth, feeling for the cord. Maybe this lighting style arose from the scarcity of furniture in a traditional house.

- Every door and window in the house slides. Over the years, my hands have learned to grasp the small recesses, carved into the door edges, which serve instead of doorknobs. There is a rather precise leverage and angle of pushing and pulling to open the doors, which can easily be derailed by a clumsy shove. Of course, I've also had to learn which doors to use, in any set of three or four, since they all move, and the wrong choice can leave a gaping hole. In addition, there's the lack of privacy—I can't lock these doors at all. Finally, sliding doors are very easy for cats to open. Most of the doorways in my house have cat-sized openings, most of the time. I just wish they would learn to close the doors!

- The Zen proverb, "In summer we sweat; in winter we shiver," is meant to illustrate the importance of not trying to escape or avoid our present situation. I have learned both the literal and symbolic truths of this proverb in my years in an ancient and drafty house. In summer, we open all the doors, and the deep eaves and porches make the house as cool as a cave when we come in sweating from farm work. In winter—well, we shiver, mostly in the kotatsu or in front of kerosene space heaters.

All this probably sounds very uncomfortable, and I guess it is. But I must admit that one of the most important gifts that Japan has given me is the ability to sit with discomfort. Stoicism—the art of getting on with the job—is well-known here. Every day in the village I meet really old people, in their 80s and 90s, who cheerfully and self-sufficiently accept discomfort and even pain as natural consequences of being alive. They seem to regard their bodies as tools for living in the world, and they use them to the full. These grannies and granddads are my role models. How important it is, indeed, to sweat in summer and shiver in winter: to accept the sand, grit and dirt of life along with the silk and sunshine, and not avoid or reject or resent them as though they were undeserved punishments.

There is a saying in Japan: *Shikata ga nai*, "It can't be helped". This saying tends to produce hoots of disbelief and derision from Westerners who have been raised on the tenet of "If you don't like it, change it". Some things, however, truly cannot be helped. Aging and death are among them. Is it possible to use the small physical discomforts—cold drafts, stubbed toes, cracking knees—as practice for the large ones which must inevitably come? If I could do that, I'd be a saint, and I'm nowhere near that state of acceptance. But the physical details of my life in Japan have gradually opened a little chink for that thought to sneak in. My body has changed, and inevitably, so has my mind.

Cash envelope offered at a funeral

Give and Take

This year, a Canadian friend organized a birthday party at her home for me and a couple of other April-born friends. When I asked her what I should bring, she answered, "You're the birthday girl. You only have to bring yourself." It was a strange feeling to arrive empty-handed at a private home—one of those times when I realized just how Japanese I've become.

The Japanese are consummate gift-givers. Presents are exchanged on every occasion, but the motive is not so much exuberant generosity as the maintaining of balance, which is an aspect of the search for harmony central to society. People are bound to each other in ever-widening circles of obligation and reciprocity, according to their positions in familial, educational, neighborhood, and employment hierarchies.

The most basic exchanges are of polite noises: ritual greetings. These are the webs of gossamer—or the cables of steel—that bind people, one to another. Phrases such as "thank you for the other day", "I'm indebted to you", "please continue your support from now on", occur again and again. When I meet someone, the difficulty of deciding which polite expression to use pales in comparison to the effort of remembering which "other day" I have to thank them for! To complicate things further, there are regional differences. A common expression of thanks in our area is *sumimasen*, which can be translated as "This will never end"—but in Tokyo this is a phrase of apology, and my Tokyo friends often say to me, "There's no need to excuse yourself all the time!"

Then there are exchanges of actual gifts. Department store food halls offer a bewildering variety of beautifully wrapped sweets, cookies, fruits, liquor, and so on, intended for presentation as gifts when visiting a private home. The homes of people more likely to be on the credit side of the ledger, such as priests, professors, and CEOs, are usually stacked to the rafters with gifts. As well, there is a special gift category, called *moraimono*, "received things"—secondhand gifts which may be exchanged among friends or relatives, thus minimizing waste.

Important occasions such as weddings, funerals, graduations, or hospitalizations usually require cash presents in special envelopes. This is easy once you're figured out how much to give. (How do we figure this out? By referring to the meticulously kept family records, of course!) These monetary gifts must be reciprocated in each case by appropriate *o-kaeshi*, return gifts. Newlyweds come back from their honeymoon laden with souvenirs for the wedding guests (who already received bags of gifts at the wedding). A person who is discharged from the hospital must give little presents to everyone who visited during the hospital stay. Guests at funerals who duly plunk down their envelopes of money at the door come away with return gifts of tea or handkerchiefs or sugar. If it seems tacky to give a present of money at a wedding or funeral, consider that the Japanese refer to cash with an honorific prefix—*o-kane*, "the honorable gold". No stigma of "filthy lucre" is attached to it.

Every foreigner living in Japan has his own horror story of the time he misinterpreted a gift or messed up the reciprocation ritual. My own humiliation occurred many years ago when some neighbors paid a call, with gift in hand of course. My mother-in-law hissed at me to find something to give them, and after frantic rummaging I produced a can of green tea which I held out with the usual self-deprecating words, "This is nothing, but please accept it." My husband shushed me and pulled me aside. These same guests had given us that very tea—from their family tea plantation!—a few weeks before. How had I missed that vital information?

So what of fellow human beings with whom we have no social connection whatsoever? I'm inclined to think that the hideous convolutions of social interaction more or less guarantee a corresponding indifference toward strangers—that this is yet another way the Japanese seek to balance their world. What a relief it must be to sit in a train surrounded by people you *don't* have to interact with, or to pass off a customer at a shop or sales department with a couple of tape-recorded polite phrases. A casual conversation between strangers at a bus stop is a very rare thing, as is extending a helping hand to a stranger in difficulty. I guess this is the feeling behind the flurry of exaggerated thanks and apologies when someone accepts a proffered seat in a train or help with luggage. After all, who wants to incur yet another potentially trouble-some debt—especially if, as in the case of strangers, it can't be paid back? Re-ciprocation is a matter of honor; to be unable to do it is shame. It must seem easier not to bother in the first place. Yet kindness, gentleness and generosity are also to be found here, like small shy animals peeping out from under the burden of social obligation. The balance is not machine-like, but, again, arises out of the organic search for harmony, one human being with another.

Every individual on this planet is a living receptacle of centuries of civilizing influence. In recent history alone, Japan endured almost three hundred years of enforced isolation, followed by upheaval, imperialism, war, and hugely accelerated industrial expansion; these elements are a heady mix roiling in the psyche. Less than two centuries ago, the social structure was so rigidly imposed that failure to conform could result in a death sentence. Of course, these days, the tinge of fear has gradually disappeared, along with, in many cases, the observances themselves. My instinct is to applaud the loosening of strictures, which might create space for true human contact; but the social framework seems to act as the moral and ethical basis of conduct. Without these rules, I wonder how the next generation will manage the fundamental need to coexist in harmony. What kinds of new practices will evolve? Will society collapse, as the older generation fears? I guess only time will tell.

Meanwhile, I have become somewhat accustomed to the rituals of social balance. Perhaps it is inevitable that my efforts seem hopelessly clumsy to the Japanese, and at the same time insanely complex and inappropriate to rela-tives and friends abroad. I'm still striving for a balance of my own, between my learned Japanese civility and the directness of Western social discourse which comes naturally. In this, as in many other areas of life, I come across as a bit strange in both cultures. Such is the predicament of the expat.

The Learning Process

My husband usually comes home from work around 8:30 p.m. First I hear the slam of the car door, then the whisper and thump of the sliding door in the entryway. Three or four footsteps, and then, at exactly the same moment every day, in exactly the same voice, he intones, *"Tadaima"* (I'm home). This phrase, which literally means "just this minute", is customarily answered by *"O-kaerinasai"* (Welcome back). Instead of this, depending on my mood, I will respond with "Hey,", "Hi", "Hello", or a simple smile. His greeting never varies; mine is never the same.

The uniformity of my husband's greeting is not due to an obsessive-compulsive personality, nor to lack of imagination. It is simply that in his culture, "Tadaima" is the thing to say when returning home. All over Japan, at countless front doors, countless homecoming people are saying the same thing. There are enormous numbers of set phrases like these in the language, covering every conceivable social contingency.

Form—the accepted way of doing things—is of great psychological importance to every Japanese. Form supports society and ensures its smooth functioning. It is the rudder that steers a crisis away from the dangerous waters of excessive emotion and into the safe haven of consensus. It is, in fact, the essential tool that can be turned to fit all life situations.

The various words for "form" are descriptive and revealing. *Shukan*, usually translated as custom, literally means "learning and getting used to", while *fushu,* manners or practices, translates as "wind-learning". (The word *fu,* wind, can itself have the meaning of "way of doing".) *Gyogi* and *reigi* (decorum) have a ritualistic nuance. There is also *furumai,* behavior, with the charming literal meaning of "waving and dancing". To instill these in their children, adults employ *shitsuke,* discipline, whose character is composed of elements meaning "the physical person" and "beautiful". Beauty is as beauty does.

If all this should seem too prettified, let me add that the Japanese themselves find the politeness of social intercourse hard to endure at times. They do have resource to a mechanism that might be viewed as hypocrisy, but hypocrisy with the moral judgment leached out of it. *Tatemae* ("wearing the mask") is essential for the smooth flow of a group activity, which might otherwise be marred—as a tapestry is flawed or a piece of blown glass bubbled— by an unseemly uncontrolled emotion or action. Later, in private, one may gossip, complain, or bad-mouth using the safety valve of *honne* or "real feelings" (which are commonly supposed to be negative). Tatemae and honne are the light and shadow of human relations in this culture; neither can exist without the other. Interestingly, real positive feelings are often described in terms that, because of their supersaturated public usage, can sound manipulative or false. Consider *fure-ai* (touching each other's heart, used to encourage participation in local events) or *kokoro wo komete* (putting one's heart into it, used in advertisements for some commercial product).

Another word for "form" is *kata* (a mold or pattern). Learning in Japan is traditionally achieved, not by absorbing verbal explanations, but by watching and imitating the actions of the teacher. In this way, essential knowledge can be transmitted without the complication of words. For the student it is essentially a matter of fitting himself into the same form as the teacher, occupying the same space, flowing through that space in the same way.

My younger son, Yuki, assimilated the forms of *kyudo,* traditional archery, over the years of high school and university. The Japanese call this process *mi ni tsuku* (attach to the body). Beginning archers are not permitted to touch an actual bow and arrow for several months, during which time they study all kinds of peripheral matters, from formal greetings to janitorial tasks, while training the muscles of their arms to assume various positions. A Westerner might be impatient with such a teaching method, especially since it brooks no questioning, short cuts or innovations. But as well as penetrating into muscle, bone, and spirit, it teaches something important—respect for the form and for the teacher who went through the same training. Here is the fountainhead of the hierarchical society: the relationship of the *sensei* (teacher, literally "born before") and the *deshi* (disciple, or "younger brother"), joined together by their devotion to the form.

Here is also the basic process of social conditioning. The Japanese mother, when her child is given something, does not merely instruct him to "say thank you"—she pushes his head down, and induces his body to bow, thus assuming the form of gratitude. These lessons "attach to the body" and are called forth instinctively in later life. Like a complicated dance, social forms, properly performed, produce an almost physical comfort of the known.

As I live here, I have begun to appreciate this feeling of comfort within a group when I demonstrate my learned ability to assume the required form. Of course I can always call upon my gaijin spontaneity and (to them) devastating honesty, but while these can be refreshing, they aren't always appropriate—they may at times interrupt the flow of the group's energy, and cause discomfort to others. What I feel, increasingly, is that there is room for both in my psyche. Why choose between these contradictory ways of self-expression? Why dogmatically insist either on my husband's unvarying greeting or on my own free-spirited approach? They are merely different steps in the great Dance of Humanity after all.

Taking Root

It's a dry, warm, still day in early November. My onion seedlings, in their month or so of early life in my front yard, have grown into sturdy green spikes about twenty centimeters high. Kneeling between them and the celery plants next door, I loosen the surrounding dirt with a trowel, and with a gentle, steady pressure, pull out the bunches of seedlings with their soft white threadlike roots. I lay them into a garden carrier and, seeing the baby roots exposed and blinking in the strong sunlight, I cover them with a powdering of soft soil. This, I hope, will ease their trundling wheelbarrow journey to my other field, five minutes' walk away.

Each rectangular bed usually holds about a hundred seedlings, planted one by one about ten centimeters apart. It may be an hour or more before the last one in the carrier is placed in the hole prepared by my burrowing gloved fingers, the hairy roots coiled underneath so as not to leave any tendrils trailing out on the surface, and finally the shoot braced with a handful of patted-down soil. At the end, my back creaking from the effort of kneeling, stretching, and moving gradually down the rows, I straighten gratefully and sprinkle first golden flakes of rice husks, and then water from a watering can, over the completed bed. The transplanting is finished—my work is done.

The work of the little onion children is just beginning. This is not the landscape of their babyhood. Where are the reassuring sheaves of celery towering nearby? No house, no car, no cats—just a flat sweep of often windy terrain, and who knows whether they can appreciate the spectacular view of the mountains. Instead of being comfortably jammed together, their intertwined roots have been untangled, and a lonely hand-span's distance now separates them. The soil here tastes different to the little clusters of roots which must now begin to explore and take hold. Through days of sunshine, clouds, rain and wind, through nights of moonlight, and later through frost and snow, the dear wish for survival pours itself from one moment to the next, as the onion children slowly adapt themselves to their new home and begin to grow.

Plants have no choices, only imperatives—and the greatest one is to survive long enough to fruit, set seed, and ensure the next generation. How graceful, how peaceful, are these little lives without choice. Clearly they want to live, but if this should prove impossible, their thread of survival thins down and down and finally disappears. With no resentment, no railing against their Maker, simple as a sigh, they rejoin the Ground of Being. I wonder what it would be like to live and die that way, without the everlasting fanfare of humanity.

It's true that for us as for every other creature, death waits. Our unique situation is that we know it, and this is the black motif in the sand painting of our day-to-day experience. But the other colors, the designs, the complexity of our lives, the brilliant flare before the dark, the dance over the abyss—all these come from choice. This is the other side of the coin of consciousness: to see beauty or not, to create or not, and ultimately, to live and die gracefully or not. The night is coming, but our choice can be the beautiful sunset.

It was choice that transplanted me. Personal choice has a size—it has limits which are imposed by society, by upbringing, by character, and by the very choices which came before. Every choice can be as small as next door or as large as across the world. Looking back, I can see the choices made by myself and others that led to this present life, so far away from the one I knew as a child. The circumstances that brought me here to Japan are infinitely more complicated than the transplanting of the onion children. Yet I like to imagine that in some way, obscure to my limited vision, it was some universal hand that dug the hole and settled me into it and patted down the soil around my fragile roots. Probably only those who have elected to be similarly transplanted could fully understand the pain, the difficulty, the complexity of the period of acclimatization which followed. And we are a small band, we transplants, a very small percentage of humanity as a whole.

Slowly, my roots went down into Japanese soil. My progress, growth, flowering, and seeding have been helped along by many others—mostly other transplants, who could reach out and feel my enduring as well as their own—friends in groups such as the Association of Foreign Wives of Japanese. I like to think that I have helped some of them too, as they put down their roots. Now, decades later, I am a strong tree, my roots are deep. I love the taste of Japanese air and water, the particular angle and strength of Japanese sunlight, the changes of Japanese seasons. I have flowered and seeded many years and hope to do so for many more. I am one of the lucky ones.

Living this way, in circumstances of otherness, gives me a deeper dimension to feel the plight of all people. All of us are transplants. All of us are uprooted, both from our mothers' wombs and, even earlier, from our Ground of Being. All of us, so many times during our lives, find our fragile roots struggling for purchase in rocky and inhospitable soil. The terrain is unfamiliar; we may at times be without the water of love or the sunshine of divinity to encourage us in our assimilation. What supports us, for a short or long time as measured on this earth, is life itself. The grand outpouring of life, its seamless and abundant flow from moment to moment, is a force so strong we are unaware of it, as the fish is unaware of water. It is this force that overrides the problems and hardships and carries us, strong and true and sure, in the direction of our destiny.

I survey the completed bed, and cheer on my onion children, starting their journey in their new home. Do your best, little seedlings! May you find everything you need for your growth.

Daruma *doll*

A Life's Work

I am spending my life in a country that is not mine by birth. This situation, or plight, or predicament, has plenty of historical precedent, and many are the words and sayings that have been invented to describe it. Am I an immigrant, an exile, a displaced person, or an alien? Am I a square peg in a round hole, a fish out of water, a rose among thorns, or a stranger in a strange land? To borrow my own metaphors, am I a homeless, malleable waif, or a vulnerable transplanted seedling? Each of these phrases has a certain ring of truth, but none of them is adequate to convey the power of free choice in the equation. I chose to come here, I chose these circumstances; I was not abducted, sold, or shanghaied into my present life. I went into it with my eyes open— maybe I didn't, or couldn't, see the whole picture, but that didn't alter the truth. This choice has had to be renewed, over the years, carved and polished into a commitment to my life.

When I first came here, adaptation was a matter of survival. Learning the language, mimicking gestures, puzzling out reactions, I was as entirely engaged as a baby trying to understand the giants around him. It was only later that I began to look around and say "Hey, wait a minute..." to some of the things I saw. Still later, it came to me that I didn't have to like everything about Japan. I had a right to decide which elements I would love, which I could live without, and which I would have to keep to a minimum in my personal life. It wasn't condemnation or judgment, but more a process of drawing the boundaries of my own adaptability. I was discovering my ada-mantine core, the part of me that holds certain things to be true, against all the bludgeoning of outside influences.

As I was evolving in my expat life, the Japanese people around me looked at me and saw a gaijin—an outsider, one who could never belong. This is the heartache of the foreigner in Japan, and it makes this a wholly differ-ent experience from that of the expat in, say, parts of Europe, or Australia. Because Japan is a group-oriented society, and because group membership is always based on commonalities rather than differences, someone who is self-evidently different can never really be a part of the group. Yet every human being is different, a precious individual, in some final way, so that a society like Japan's offers its individual members two choices. They can squeeze and restrict themselves in order to fit in, or they can remain proudly individual, relinquishing the privileges of the group. The Japanese have learned to live within the stern limits of these choices. There are some notable exceptions, but generally speaking, they obey their learned dread of aloneness and take refuge in the undoubted but stultifying comfort that the group offers.

I can see these alternatives clearly, precisely because I am an outsider, and I have felt in my heart the painful vacillation between longing to fit in and holding myself aloof. These may seem mutually exclusive, but on consider-ation, they begin to reveal themselves as illusory and even complementary. It is a dynamic stasis, like opposing forces, that suspend each human being in the precise relationship to the society that he can live with from day to day. This is a universal truth about social man. It's just that in Japan, the psy-chological distance between the group and the individual is greater, and the consequences of a final choice more dire.

So how would I describe my life as it is now? I think the most appropri-ate symbol is that homely and ubiquitous figure, the Daruma doll. A cheap, red-and-white papier-mache figurine of varying size, little more than a blank-eyed, scowling bearded face painted onto a roly-poly body, Daruma is a folk character that presides over new ventures. When one begins a project, one paints in one of the eyes, and the other when the project is successfully com-pleted. Daruma is rounded and weighted on the bottom, so that it may lean to one side or the other—but it always rights itself, true to the Daruma slogan *Nana-korobi, ya-oki* ("Fall down seven times, get up eight times"). The lofty inspiration for this folk character was the formidable Indian Buddhist monk Bodhidharma, who is said to have sat so long in meditation that his legs fell off—the epitome of grim determination and single-mindedness. I'm not sure how single-minded I am, but it's true that I have often felt myself leaning, buffeted by the winds of the society around me, only to return to the vertical of my heart's truth again and again.

So here's the conundrum: Is my real self the one that leans to accommodate outside forces, or the one that springs upright when these forces abate? A Japanese person would no doubt label these two extremes in the opposite way, seeing his individual whims as the leaning phase, and his realignment with the pole star of his group as the return to the vertical. This is the clue to the solution of the riddle. I am reminded of a time when I went to see a counselor. At our first meeting, she asked me, "Do you ever see things that aren't really there?" This struck me as a ridiculous question, and I responded, "How do I know what's really there?" In the same way, my "real" self is not to be found in any arbitrary set of parameters, imposed either from without or from within. The Daruma doll sometimes leans, and sometimes stands upright, but remains itself throughout. Thus I must be as well.

For my identity to be honest, my acceptance of myself must include both the leaning and the standing tall: it must be total. Further, ideally, I must practice acceptance in a mood of friendship, tolerance and cooperation. I am of course free to notice where there is room for improvement, and to make efforts in this direction as they are in my power; but I cannot turn away, I cannot condemn or abandon any part. And my acceptance of every part of myself is mirrored in my outer life, as I endeavor to accept every part of my adopted country, Japan. I make friends with the weakness, inconsistency, and ugliness of Japan, as well as the inimitable beauty and limitless richness to be found here, at the same time as I am learning to do the same within myself. That's how I am discovering my identity. It seems that is my life's work.

A Glossary of Japanese Terms

A

amae	feeling of comfortable dependence
amai	sweet, easy
Atago-ko	group of families associated with Atago Shrine in Kyoto

B

bengara	rust-colored iron oxide pigment used to treat wood
Bon-Odori	summer dance at O-bon festival, usually performed outside at night
butsudan	Buddha-cabinet or household Buddhist altar

D

daifuku-mochi	round white sweet filled with bean paste or fruit
daruma	figurine designed to bring good fortune, based on Buddhist saint Bodhidharma
deshi	student or disciple

F

~fu	way of doing something
fue	traditional side flute
fure-ai	touch each other's heart
furumai	behavior
fushu	manners, practice
fusuma	interior sliding doors with thick paper on both sides

G

gaijin	foreigner, outsider
go-en	five yen; also, fortune or connection
gochiso	feast, elaborate meal for guests
gyogi	decorum, manners

H

hana	flower; can refer specifically to cherry blossom
hanafuda	flower cards, a traditional card game
hanami-dango	colored round sweets eaten while viewing cherry blossoms

haru	spring
hashioki	chopstick rest
higan-bana	"equinox flower" or spider lily
higashi	dry, crumbly or pressed sweets
honne	true feelings, expressed in private
hotoke-sama	Buddha, or a deceased person

I

isogashii	busy

J

jimi	subdued (e.g., dress color)
jugyo	lesson

K

kamidana	god-shelf for housing Shinto offerings
kanarazu	without fail
kanten	transparent gelatin
kasutera	pound cake originally from Portugal
kata	form, pattern
kawaiku nai	unloveable
kawa-no-ji	sleeping arrangement of mother, baby, and father, mimicking the character for "river"
koban	gold piece shaped like a rice bale, used in feudal times
kokeshi	wooden doll
kokoro	heart
kokoro wo komete	put one's heart into it
koma-inu	lion-dog, originating in China, protective deity of shrines
konpeito	colored rock sugar, originally from Portugal
koromogae	changing clothes, also seasonal changing of doors in a house
korosu	kill
kotatsu	low table, sometimes recessed into the floor, with built-in heater and blanket
koto	traditional floor harp
kotobuki	congratulatory character meaning "long life"
kuruma	wheeled vehicle
kyoiku	education
kyudo	traditional archery

M

mainichi-benkyo	every day a learning experience
mainichi-shiken	every day an examination
maru	circle; round; goodness
maru-arai	washing and renewing a futon
meibutsu-gashi	specialty sweets of a region
mi ni tsuku	physically based method of learning
miso	fermented, salty paste made from rice or beans, used in cooking
miyabi	gorgeousness
momiji-gari	tourism based on going to view autumn colors of maple trees
mono no aware	Japanese aesthetic based on the sadness of impermanence

N

naginata	long sword mainly used by women
nana-korobi ya-oki	"seven times down, eight times up" motto of Daruma figurine

O

(Hyphenated "o" at the beginning of a word is an honorific prefix.)

obachan	auntie; affectionate term for an older woman
O-Bon	summer festival when deceased family members are thought to visit the living
o-furo	bath
O-Jizo	patron saint of travelers and children; shrines are usually placed at the boundaries of a village
o-kaeri-nasai	"Welcome home"
o-kane	"honorable gold" i.e., cash money
okorinbo	hot-tempered person
o-mamori	charm for a safe journey
o-mochi	glutinous rice dough used in ceremonies and sweet-making
omogashi	"main" or heavy sweets with a moist or sticky consistency
o-motenashi	hospitality
o-shiruko	hot sweet soup made from red beans
o-tsuki-mi	moon-viewing
owaru	end, finish
oya-gawari	person who stands in for a parent at a ceremony

o-zoni	New Year soup with regionally varied ingredients, but always containing o-mochi

R

rakugo	traditional comic monologue
reigi	decorum

S

sakaki	paulownia, sacred tree of Shinto
sake	rice wine
sakura	cherry tree, cherry blossom
sakura-mochi	sweet made with salted cherry leaf
sakura-zensen	"cherry blossom front"; term used by weathermen to describe the south-to-north movement of blooming in spring
sashimi	sliced raw fish
seken no me	"Eye of the World"; social judgment which acts as curb on behavior
senbei-buton	an old, thin, flat futon, jokingly called "rice-cracker"
sensei	teacher
shakuhachi	bamboo recorder-like wind instrument
shikata ga nai	"it can't be helped"
shimai-buro	the last bath of the evening
shimenawa	New year decoration, hung on lintels and sometimes cars
shitsuke	discipline
sho-chiku-bai	pine, bamboo, plum—congratulatory symbols
shoji	sliding door made of a wooden lattice with paper glued on
shoki	protector deity
shukan	custom
sumo	traditional wrestling

T

ta	rice paddy
tabi	socks with big toe separated, worn with kimono
tadaima	"I'm home"
tagai	mutuality
taihen desu ne	"That's a lot to bear"—expression of commiseration

takenoko	bamboo shoots
tatami	thick woven straw mats, flooring for most Japanese rooms
tategu	sliding doors
tatemae	"wearing the mask", polite discourse in public
Tekka matsuri	local festival commemorating 1619 trial by fire
tokonoma	alcove, raising part of a room used for decoration and offering
tonari-gumi	block of families in village or town, local unit of management
torii	gate of a shrine
toshi-koshi-soba	"year-crossing noodles", buckwheat noodles eaten on New Year's Eve
tsuru-kame	crane and turtle—congratulatory symbols

U

uma	horse

W

wa	harmony
wabi-sabi	Japanese aesthetic of poverty, plainness and irregular shape
warui kao	unpleasant or negative facial expression

Y

yagura	decorated wooden platform or tower for performing musicians
yugen	Japanese aesthetic of remoteness, loneliness, otherworldliness
yukata	cotton summer kimono
yuzu	a citrus fruit

Z

zori	slippers worn with kimono